NEVER MAKE
THE FIRST OFFER

NEVER MAKE THE FIRST OFFER

(EXCEPT WHEN YOU SHOULD)
WISDOM FROM A MASTER
DEALMAKER

DONALD DELL

WITH JOHN BOSWELL

PORTFOLIO

PORTFOLIO

Published by the Penguin Group

Penguin Group (USA) Inc., 375 Hudson Street, New York, New York 10014, U.S.A.
Penguin Group (Canada), 90 Eglinton Avenue East, Suite 700, Toronto, Ontario,
Canada M4P 2Y3 (a division of Pearson Penguin Canada Inc.)
Penguin Books Ltd, 80 Strand, London WC2R 0RL, England
Penguin Ireland, 25 St Stephen's Green, Dublin 2, Ireland (a division of Penguin Books Ltd)
Penguin Books Australia Ltd, 250 Camberwell Road, Camberwell, Victoria 3124, Australia
(a division of Pearson Australia Group Pty Ltd)
Penguin Books India Pvt Ltd, 11 Community Centre,
Panchsheel Park, New Delhi – 110 017, India
Penguin Group (NZ), 67 Apollo Drive, Rosedale, North Shore 0632, New Zealand
(a division of Pearson New Zealand Ltd)
Penguin Books (South Africa) (Pty) Ltd, 24 Sturdee Avenue, Rosebank,
Johnnesburg 2196, South Africa

Penguin Books Ltd, Registered Offices: 80 Strand, London WC2R 0RL, England

First published in 2009 by Portfolio, a member of Penguin Group (USA) Inc.

1   3   5   7   9   10   8   6   4   2

Copyright © Donald Dell and John Boswell, 2009
All rights reserved

Library of Congress Cataloging-in-Publication Data
Dell, Donald L.
Never make the first offer : (except when you should) wisdom from a master dealmaker /
Donald Dell with John Boswell.
p.   cm.
Includes index.
ISBN 978-1-59184-265-1
1. Deals.   I. Boswell, John.   II. Title.
HD58.6.D45 2009
658.4'052—dc22   2009010611

Printed in the United States of America
Set in Legacy Serif
Designed by Jaime Putorti

To my love, Carole, my wonderful partner, who inspires me always.
To my exceptional daughters, Alexandra and Kristina, whose talents
and love are the source of our pride and joy.
And to my mother, Margaret (Gaga), who possesses the spirit and
determination I have always tried to emulate.

CONTENTS

ACKNOWLEDGMENTS

I would like to acknowledge the enormous help given to me in creating this book. First, my sincere thanks and appreciation to John Boswell for his vision and the nature and content of this book. Without his effort and long hours of work, it would not have been written, because John was the driving force in putting it all together.

I would also like to thank my publisher, Adrian Zackheim of Portfolio, whose support and belief contributed to the book's final product, and Courtney Young, whose skillful and caring editing made it a better, more interesting read. Also, my sincere thanks to Emily Winter, John's assistant, for her many contributions in organizing the material, and my appreciation to my wife, Carole, for her editing and attention to detail.

In particular, I want to thank my colleagues at our new company, BEST, Inc. (Blue Entertainment Sports Television), Jeff

Newman, John Tobias, Chris Martin, Sam Duvall, and Blair Giles for their support and encouragement in our daily work.

I am very grateful to Dennis Spencer, my partner for twenty-five years and the Head of BEST TV, for his thoughtful review of every anecdote told in the book and for his friendship.

To my executive assistant, Margaret Van Milder, and administrative assistant, Karen Salter, my thanks for their tireless dedication and skill in "keeping it all together."

Finally, my special thanks to my partner and chairman of BEST, Inc., Jonathan Blue, for his hard work, balanced judgment, and sense of fairness, which empowers me to strive for excellence in our business activities.

NEVER MAKE
THE FIRST OFFER

THE MOMENT OF TRUTH

I had been stuck in a tense negotiation with the chief operating officer and several other executives of a company called AMF, which made Head tennis rackets, for what seemed like hours, when the conference room door suddenly flew open.

I expected the renegotiation of tennis star Arthur Ashe's Head racket deal to go smoothly. Head was a ski equipment company that had just made a great amount of money selling the very first graphite tennis racket with Arthur's endorsement. The new material and snowshoe shape were far superior to wooden rackets and sold for more than twice their price. Head now made seven different graphite models, and my client, Arthur—who had his name on the original model—had been receiving a 5 percent royalty on all of them. But AMF, which had recently bought out Head, said they were finished paying Arthur royalties.

The COO and I had been cordial but firm on our stances: I pushed for Arthur's royalties, and he refused. We were at a complete impasse until that door swung open and the chairman of AMF came storming in. Pierre (I'll refer to him only by his first name) was so angry that I could see the veins popping out of his neck.

"Goddamnit!" he screamed. "We're not paying Ashe any more royalties. This is outrageous. He's making ten times what I'm making, and I'm chairman of this company!"

The silence was deafening and palpable. Tension filled the room. After a moment of shock, everyone turned to me to see what I would do next.

These are the moments I live for.

This is when the instincts of a true dealmaker really come into play. All the preparation and all the hard work had been done, and now the moment of truth had arrived. It was pass or fail, and the decision was largely in my hands.

I suppose you could say that I am a born dealmaker. In fact, back when I was a color commentator at Wimbledon for NBC, my broadcasting partner, Bud Collins, would tease me by calling me "Donald Deal" over the air, as in, "Donald, it's eight a.m. back on the East Coast. So how many deals have you done today?" Or, "Donald, I guess I can't accuse you of conflict of interest today because in this match you represent both players."

Still, there is nothing in my background to suggest I would go on to represent a who's who in the world of sports including Arthur, Stan Smith, Michael Jordan, Pudge Rodriguez, Patrick Ewing, Jimmy Connors, Andy Roddick, and about three hundred other world-class athletes.

Except for one thing: I have always been supercompetitive.

Even as a kid I was ranked number one in U.S. Junior Tennis, and when I got a little older, I managed to make it as far as the quarterfinals of the U.S. Open Championships.

The reason I've always loved tennis is its competitive ethic. You go out, usually one-on-one, and try to beat the other guy's brains out. Then, win or lose, you go up to the net and shake hands.

I suppose the parallel in business is making deals. You do everything you can for your client or for your company. Then, if it's going to be a good deal for everyone, you need to be able to go to the net and shake hands.

When I started out, I was captain of the U.S. Davis Cup team just as tennis was about to turn professional. My two best players were Stan Smith and Arthur Ashe. I already had my law degree and was looking forward to working in a big firm and becoming a successful litigator. But then Arthur said, "Why don't you represent me?" That's what led me to found ProServ, one of the first sports management companies, and started me on a lifetime of dealmaking.

Everything I know has been the result of on-the-job training, learn as you go. And when it comes to dealmaking, I feel I've learned a lot. Now, after doing this for forty years, I'd like to share everything I've learned with you. Because what I can pass on is based on real people and real events, I think in many ways it is more valuable than anything you're going to get out of a negotiating class in business school. Among the subjects to be covered are: the keys to great networking, how to win before you even begin, how to develop leverage for yourself, how to take advantage of what others may accidentally give you, and, of course, how to close the deal. I also believe you can learn more from your failures than from your successes, and I have shared plenty of both in this book.

Sports can also be a dirty business, with people going back on their word, lying, cheating, and stealing—and that's just the expected thing. I've included some stories here that will reveal the seamier side of sports as well. It is shocking what people will do when a lot of money is on the line, and I'm not someone who is easily shocked.

In addition to representing many prominent people, I have also had the opportunity over the years to turn a number of my business relationships into friendships. Many of these friends, some with familiar names, are or were at the top of their professions. While writing this book it occurred to me that it might be interesting to get their perspective on the dealmaking process as well. So interspersed among my stories (and set off from the rest of the text) are their responses to the question: "What do you think is the most important aspect of a deal?" I think you will find many of their answers provocative.

Now back to Pierre. When we left off, Pierre had just walked into the room and announced that he was no longer willing to pay royalties to Arthur Ashe that were substantially more than Pierre made, because he was the chairman of the company. One of the obvious rules of negotiating is to keep emotions out of the process. So, once Pierre had given this ultimatum, it was obviously too late for that. My job was to try not to respond in kind and to try to lower the temperature in the room.

Moreover, Pierre's argument was completely bogus. In fact, the more royalties they paid to Arthur, the more rackets they were selling. And the more money the company made, the more likely the board of directors would be generous with Pierre. In reality, Pierre should have been making the exact opposite argument. But none of that mattered now. There were eight or nine people in the room, and they were all looking at me to see how I was going to respond. There was dead silence, and you could feel the tension. After thinking for a moment—and I don't know where this came from or why it occurred to me—I said, "But Pierre, Arthur has a much better serve than you do."

Everyone laughed, and the tension in the room was immediately broken. We ended up accepting a smaller royalty, but we did get a royalty *and* we kept the relationship going.

1

TEN RULES OF POWER NETWORKING

In 1937 a man by the name of Dale Carnegie wrote a book entitled *How to Win Friends and Influence People,* which went on to become the best-selling self-help book of all time. It was intended primarily as a book on personal growth, yet more than seventy years later it remains among the top fifty titles on the business best-seller list. Why? Because all things being equal, people like to do business with their friends; and all things not being equal, people still like to do business with friends.

By "friends" I don't mean your buddies from back in high school. More often than not that can be a loaded situation. What I do mean is that there is probably nothing more fundamental to good business than building long-lasting relationships—dealing with the people you know and like and who know and like you.

One of the most well liked men in the sports business today is Under Armour's young founder, Kevin Plank. Like many "overnight" success stories, Under Armour was actually founded twelve years ago but flew under the radar for a good seven years before it really started to take off and began showing up in sporting goods stores and gyms with the same ubiquity as older, more established brands such as Nike, Adidas, and Reebok.

Today Under Armour is a $750 million company, and recently I had the opportunity to talk to Kevin over breakfast. When I asked him to what he attributed his success, he said, "Relationships. It's all about relationships—meeting people, treating them with decency and dignity, and turning them into friends."

Kevin told me how he had started his company one relationship at a time. He said he didn't have any business connections whatsoever when he was a football player at the University of Maryland. Still, his goal was to start his own business selling compression T-shirts to university athletic programs. Kevin did have a good relationship with his equipment manager, and one day he asked him whom he should talk to about his business plan. The equipment manager said, "You should be talking to me."

Most people assume that equipment managers are responsible just for washing the jocks and laying out the clothes every day, but as it turned out, this "lowly" equipment guy controlled an annual budget of $650,000! He explained to Kevin that that was how it worked throughout the Atlantic Coast Conference (ACC), and because Kevin had always treated the equipment manager with respect, he agreed to introduce him to other equipment managers from the ACC. Kevin took his performance apparel on the road, building relationships with other equipment managers and attending their annual conventions. At the conventions he would take eight to ten managers out for dinner and drinks.

Kevin had gone to high school at Fork Union Military Academy, a school known for developing football players into college and pro material. In his class alone, twenty-three players went to Division I schools, including future Heisman Trophy winner Eddie George. Of the twenty-three Division I college players, thirteen ended up turning pro. That was the beginning of Kevin's entrée into professional sports.

He said he never asked any of his former classmates to plug the shirts on his behalf, but what he did do was send them free shirts and say, "Let me know what you think, and if you like them, give some to the guys in the lockers next to you." Then he'd call their equipment managers and say, "You might have seen some of your players wearing our compression T-shirts. They're superior to anything else out there, and I'd like to come down and talk to you about them."

Today Under Armour is in contact with most of the Division I teams and professional teams throughout the National Football League, the National Basketball Association, the National Hockey League, and Major League Baseball. It is these connections that drive the retail sales in sporting goods stores and fitness clubs, and these connections were initially built one equipment manager at a time.

Kevin told me, "When people ask me if I am surprised by the success we have achieved, I often say, 'I've always been smart enough to be naïve enough to not know what I couldn't accomplish.' And what we have accomplished is directly attributable to the friends we've made and the relationships we have built and maintained."

Rule #1: Make Friends

Kevin Plank's secret isn't just that he's a nice guy. He worked at every relationship—and not just by scheduling business meetings on the road. What Kevin has done, and what I think is the most basic aspect of achieving business success, is to create opportunities to get to know people *out* of the office, out of the normal parameters of the business relationship, and outside mutual comfort zones. When you are away from the negotiating table, it is incredible how much people start to open up. And it's surprising how much fun you can have.

What you have to remember is to be informal, not to have an agenda, and not expect instant rewards for befriending people in your field of business. It takes time, and a friendship will only work if you're *natural* and *consistent*. It is the ultimate test in people skills. When you make friends with one or two people, a whole network of professional contacts will become apparent and available to you.

With many of my best business contacts, it actually hasn't

taken a whole lot of effort to turn the relationship into something more personal, because following these rules eventually becomes second nature. The process usually begins with what I would describe as a "defining moment," some sort of shared experience (often humorous) that takes place outside the normal business comfort zone. With Horst Dassler, head of Adidas, it began with an invitation from British track star and go-between John Boulter—not to Horst's office (or to the restaurant he also owned) but to his home for dinner in Landersheim, France.

Horst lived on a magnificent seventeenth-century estate. After being treated to a delicious dinner, I retired with him and three of his business associates to another room for cognac and cigars. Horst and I had talked well into the night, when all of a sudden we realized that we were the only ones doing the talking. His three business associates, still sitting straight up in their chairs, had all fallen asleep! I guess that we two blowhards putting everyone else asleep was a defining moment in our relationship.

Adidas had been founded by Horst's father, Adi Dassler (Adi + Dassler = Adidas). Adidas was the biggest name in sports in Germany and the biggest name in soccer in the world, but Horst was fed up with sharing the company with his four sisters, so he moved to France. There he took Adidas into other sports, such as track and field and tennis; other countries, including America; and other merchandise, such as apparel (the beginning of Adidas's iconic three stripes). In five years he outgrew what remained of Adidas in Germany tenfold. Horst was the smartest sports marketer I've ever dealt with. He was also on the other end of my first company's first deal.

The first deal I ever made for ProServ was for tennis star Stan Smith. Today it seems that every superstar athlete has his or her own shoe deal, but back then it was unheard-of. The most lucrative tennis shoe licensing deal ever was Stan Smith's deal with Adidas, beginning in 1972.

Shortly after my cigar and cognac night with Horst, Stan Smith won his first Wimbledon title. The very next day I received a call from Horst, who said, "I want to sign Stan Smith."

After a moment of hesitation I said, "You can't afford him." I knew that would infuriate Horst, which it did, and make him want Stan even more, which it also did. I had already put Stan in a package deal for shoes with other American players endorsing Converse. The contracts hadn't been signed yet, but I knew that if I pulled Stan out of the package, there would be hell to pay (Converse didn't speak to me for three years), so it had to be worth it.

"Okay," I said, "but I want a five percent royalty on all Smith/Adidas shoes."

Horst went ballistic, but I knew what his goals were: Stan was his ticket into America. So after a lot of back-and-forth he eventually agreed. Neither of us knew at the time how big Adidas would become in this country, so it was sort of like dealing with play money. (Soon after this I would use the same approach in making that incredibly lucrative deal for Arthur Ashe with then-unknown Head rackets.)

Of course, making friends isn't about pulling information out of people over cognac. If you go into a dinner with that kind of goal, it will be transparent, and no one will warm up to you. Be authentic. Find commonalities between you and your soon-to-be friend. Get comfortable and sincerely enjoy yourself.

The first time I got to know Phil Knight, the founder and CEO of Nike, I completely didn't see it coming, and that's how it should always be. You can't force a friendship, just as you can't force a deal.

Both Phil and I were in Rome with our wives, Penny and Carole, for the Italian Open. On this particular day a steady light rain was falling, and by early afternoon all the matches had been canceled. Phil and I didn't know each other very well, but the four of us decided to look for a place to have lunch together. We found this perfect little café where we could sit outside under an awning. It was still misting, and the whole atmosphere was Italian, intimate, and very sensual.

Basically what happened is that the four of us sat there for about five hours and proceeded to get very drunk. There is nothing like a few bottles of wine "among friends" to quickly break down barriers, and by early evening I had gone from barely knowing Phil to feeling I could talk to him about almost anything.

A few years later we would do what might be considered the most famous licensing deal in the history of sports: the deal with Nike for Air Jordan.

Horst Dassler and Phil Knight essentially controlled the athletic shoe business throughout the 1980s and 1990s. We would deal with their companies many times, though rarely with Horst or Phil directly. But we didn't have to. Almost everyone we dealt with at

Adidas and Nike knew that I had more than a business-as-usual relationship with their boss. And in both cases I can trace back when the casual friendship began to a specific shared experience.

Rule #2: Make Friends of Their Friends

One of the great opening lines to a business encounter is: "So-and-so suggested I call." It gives you immediate credibility and opens the door to a potential new working relationship. Maybe this is just another way to emphasize the importance of networking, but whenever I need to get to someone I don't know, my first thought is, "Who do I know that they know?" Simply by introducing you, that person is giving you a recommendation. What is less recognized is that it is also a kind of insurance policy. Most people aren't going to risk their prior existing relationships just to try to screw you in a deal or not live up to their end of the bargain. There have been occasions when I could have reached someone directly but went through a mutual friend because of the protection it offered.

It's a small world after all—a fact that I've been able to use to my advantage in business. "Six degrees of separation" is a commonly used phrase which means that if you are one degree of separation away from everyone you know, and two degrees away from everyone they know, and so on, you are only six degrees away from anyone in the world you might want to be in touch with. Confined just to business, I'm convinced that I can reach anyone I want to know—and probably you can, too—in three degrees of separation: a friend of a friend of a friend.

I originally met Fred Smith, founder and CEO of Federal Express, through my friend Billy Dunavant, who had owned the Memphis Racquet Club in Tennessee and is also the biggest independent cotton broker in the world. Billy had set up a doubles match with Fred and another friend named Mac Winkler, and me. But, since a tournament was being held at Billy's club and since it was the dead of winter, he had to find another indoor facility. As it turned out, the only other courts available were all hard courts.

Fred was actually quite good, and as soon as I saw him hit a few balls, I said, "I want you to be my partner." The match had barely begun, when a ball was hit down the line, and Fred dove for it—I mean he was literally airborne—on this very hard court.

"What are you doing?" I said. "You're going to kill yourself."

"What do you mean, 'What am I doing?'" he replied. "I'm trying to win the point!"

We both laughed, but the game revealed his competitive drive, the drive that had made FedEx such a spectacular success. We remained friends, and I ended up representing FedEx twenty years later in the $205 million deal to rename the Washington Redskins stadium FedExField (the biggest naming rights deal in the NFL up to that time).

Rule #3: Find Mentors

One of the most flattering things you can do for someone is ask him for advice. As much as I like to give advice, I like to receive it even more, only I call it coaching. Whenever I go into a meeting or a negotiation and don't know all the facts or the personalities in the room, and someone else does, I will say, "Give me some coaching." Obviously, the more I know, the more it is to my advantage.

There are two main mentors in my life. One is the tennis great Jack Kramer. The other one, who has taught me everything I know about people skills, is the politician and activist Robert Sargent Shriver Jr., affectionately known as Sarge. Although meeting Sarge was easy (he called me up one day when I was in my twenties and asked me to coach his son Bobby in tennis), I didn't become his protégé by waiting for him to mentor me. I had to ask.

Soon after I started teaching Bobby tennis, Sarge offered me a job with a fairly new program he helped launch, the Peace Corps. I had a new job at a Washington law firm, so I turned him down but kept my friendly contact with the family. A few years later Sarge invited me to their Cape Cod home to play tennis with the family and have a relaxing weekend. One Saturday, when I was on a boat waterskiing with John Kennedy's sister, Pat Lawford, she asked me where I worked, and I told her I was a lawyer at a firm called Hogan & Hartson. She asked me what I wanted to do with my life. Was my goal to make partner?

Back at the house while everyone was taking an afternoon nap, I lay awake. I knew I did not want to be a partner in a law firm, but I was headed directly for that kind of job. I wandered into the living room of the silent house and found Sarge reading a book. Here's where I got nervous: I knew Sarge liked me, but I had turned down a job with him once already. I wasn't sure if I should ask him for help or advice, but I knew it was better to try and fail than to keep silent. I asked Sarge if he would reopen his offer.

He said yes immediately. He told me he would be taking over as head of the Office of Economic Opportunity, and I could choose one of three jobs: as one of their lawyers, as a recruiter on college campuses, or as his assistant, his right-hand man. While the first two jobs sounded very interesting, I realized I had the unique opportunity to build a lifelong mentorship with Sarge by being his assistant. Sarge is still alive at ninety-three, and he's still one of my greatest mentors and a close friend.

Rule #4: Give Advice (Carefully)

Another way to build friendships is by offering advice—as long as it has either been solicited or is couched in such in a way that you don't come across as a know-it-all or a big shot.

I tend to offer advice whether it's asked for or not. (Stan Smith teases me that the only helpful advice I ever gave him was "Get your first serve in.") But I have found that if it is offered in

USE YOUR SUPPORT SYSTEM
Bill Bradley

Bradley is an American Hall of Fame basketball player, Rhodes scholar, former U.S. senator from New Jersey, and presidential candidate who ran for the Democratic Party's nomination for president in the 2000 election.

When I was in the U.S. Senate, the most important aspect of closing a deal was to listen carefully to what the other side was really saying so that any counterproposal you offered would address exactly what the other side really cared about.

If the deal doesn't work out, it is good to have the ability to say no nicely—no histrionics, no feigned anger, just the facts and your position in relation to them. If you say no, don't make the person on the other side of the table angry. Make him sorry that you weren't able to get a deal at that time. This way you leave open the possibility of getting a deal in the future, which would not be the case if the meeting ended with mutual acrimony.

And, finally, remember to use your support system. During the Tax Reform Act of 1986, we got to a crucial moment on the last day when Treasury Secretary Jim Baker needed a particular addition to the bill and the congressional negotiators didn't think we could give it. We knew that the deal was either going to be made or broken in the next hour. I left the meeting, made a call to my tax guru, told him Baker's problem, and he offered a solution. I returned to the committee room, offered the solution, and Baker said that it would meet the need. We had a deal. That result would never have happened had I not been prepared with the right support available at the right time. ■

such a way that the other person knows I am genuinely trying to be helpful, it is usually appreciated.

I have known Ken Chenault, whom I met through Arthur Ashe, since he was a fast-rising executive at American Express. I once said to him, "American Express has gotten too old and too fat. You should be dominating, but Visa is eating your lunch. You're like this sleeping giant."

Several years later, after Ken Chenault had become the CEO of American Express, I visited his office, and the first thing he said to me was, "The sleeping giant has awakened!"

I couldn't believe that he had remembered my comment, but I was, very flattered that he had. This was one time when an unasked-for piece of advice seems to have been appreciated. Later we would do the Andy Roddick deal with American Express. To this day I don't know if Ken Chenault was directly involved—probably not—but if we had needed his help, I'm sure he would have been there to give us a hand.

Rule #5: Don't Keep Score

Don't keep track of favors asked or favors given. Doing someone a favor is like money in the bank—as long as you don't try to collect right away.

Just as I often ask myself, "Who do I know that he knows?" there are people out there who often ask themselves, "Who does he know that I want to know?" Whenever someone asks you for a business favor, jump on it. It is an opportunity, not an obligation. But here's the main point about expanding your business circle: Expect nothing in return.

Don't keep score. Dealmaking and business in general ride on the backs of favors offered, favors done, and favors returned, but if you ever try to consciously balance the scorecard, people are more likely to remember that than the favor you might have done for them in the first place.

Allow the business gods to even the score. In my experience, if you do the right thing and expect nothing in return, to paraphrase John Lennon, business karma will come to you. In fact, I had this one experience where it took an entire generation!

The story begins in Africa over thirty-five years ago. I had received a phone call from Arthur Ashe, who was in Cameroon on a goodwill tour of Africa. "Donald," he said, "you wouldn't believe this kid I just hit with. He may be the most natural tennis player I've ever seen."

This talented thirteen-year-old had literally carved a racket out of a tree—it looked like a giant Ping-Pong paddle—yet he had held his own hitting against Arthur, who was then the number two player in the world. At Arthur's behest I called Philippe Chatrier, president of the French Tennis Federation. The French had a wonderful program for gifted kids that gave them the best training in the world and also provided a great education, all expenses paid. I had been friends with Philippe for a long time (he was a great friend of Jack Kramer, my best friend in tennis), and as a favor to me he agreed to support this kid from Cameroon.

That young prodigy was Yannick Noah, one of the most graceful and beautiful players to ever pick up a tennis racket. Yannick was in the top ten for almost a decade, but his crowning achievement was in 1983, when he won the French Open, the last Frenchman to do so. Yannick was always so grateful for what Arthur and I had done for him.

Fast-forward to 2007. Yannick Noah has a new career and is now the most famous singer in France and, according to a recent poll, also France's most popular personality. Meanwhile, I had gone through some career changes of my own. After founding ProServ in 1970, I sold it in 1998. Then I had the opportunity to buy it back again for twenty cents on the dollar, which I did in partnership with Jonathan Blue, a venture capitalist who owns our new parent, Blue Equity. I had been drifting toward retirement, but I found out that I missed the thrill of the chase too much. I was anxious to start making deals again.

Around this time I received a call from Yannick. We had kept in touch over the years, but this time he said, "Donald, Joakim has decided to leave the University of Florida and turn pro." (Joakim is Yannick's son, and he won the NCAA basketball tournament's MVP award in 2006.) "His mother, Cecilia, and I want you to represent him." Yannick had always been very appreciative of everything I had done for him as his lawyer and friend, and this was coming back to me at a perfect time.

Several weeks later I was talking to Joakim on the phone, and he said, "Donald, you should also represent my roommate, Corey Brewer." (He won the NCAA's MVP in 2007.) "Here, let me put him on the phone."

The NBA draft is very stressful if you have a rooting interest, which I obviously had, but Corey was picked number seven and Joakim was picked number nine, thus assuring both of them financial security for the rest of their lives. I could never have foreseen that day when I called Philippe Chatrier, and how it would come back to me. It was threefold in blessings.

Rule #6: Massage Your Network

Keep the cards and letters and emails going out. "Out of sight, out of mind" is just as true in business as it is in life.

Recently I read the front-cover profile of Arnon Milchan in *Cigar Aficionado*. Although Arnon is one of the most powerful movie producers in the world (*Pretty Woman, L.A. Confidential,* and about fifty others), and although we have rarely done business together, I immediately dropped him a note telling him how great I thought the article was.

The point is that I immediately heard back from him. Whenever I drop someone a note because their name has come up in a conversation or I have seen something written about them, they invariably get back to me, which keeps the relationship going. Arnon is such a world traveler that I had no idea where he was calling from, but before he hung up, we discovered we were going to be in Paris at the same time and agreed to have dinner together.

The quality of your network is only as good as your ability to keep it fresh. Email has now made doing so a no-brainer, but I am still fond of the personal touch of a handwritten note.

It is also the reason I continue to pay for courtside boxes at maybe a dozen tennis tournaments around the world, including Wimbledon, the French Open, and the U.S. Open.

At the 2008 U.S. Open, David Stern—commissioner of the NBA—and his wife, Diane, who loves tennis, were scheduled to be among my guests at the finals. But the Sunday finals were rained out and rescheduled for the following Monday. I received a nice message from David saying he would not be able to attend the rescheduled match. That would have been the end of it, but it occurred to me that perhaps Diane would like to come anyway. In fact, I also saw it as an opportunity to needle David, and I left her a message to that effect. I said, "I know David can't come, but I'd love to have you come without him." Ultimately, she couldn't make it, but she made a point of calling back and telling me what a kick both she and David got out of my message.

Rule #7: Do Your Homework

Whether it is the details of a deal or a business contact, know whatever is knowable before going to the negotiating table. It is the little facts that impress the most, and if you don't learn them, someone else will.

As the saying goes, "Some days you get the bear, and some days the bear gets you." I remember this one particular time when I was definitely gotten by the bear—or, more accurately, a recruiter named Tom Collins—and it was too late for me to do much about it.

I was good friends with the basketball coach of the University of Virginia (my law school alma mater), Terry Holland, or at least good enough friends to have been invited to his office to meet with Ralph Sampson and his mother. The seven-foot-tall Sampson (back when seven feet was still considered tall) was the best college player in the country that year and was sure to be number one in the NBA draft. I was very confident about our chances of representing him. We had the most stellar list of basketball clients in the country, and we knew how to make a persuasive presentation, which we did.

After the meeting I said to Terry, "I think that went really well."

He said, "He's not going to sign with you."

We were shocked, and I asked him how he could be so sure. "Because," he said, "his mother didn't invite you home to dinner like she did with the guy that was in here yesterday."

He ended up being right, of course.

I love to compete and I hate to lose, but even Roger Federer loses a match every now and then. What you need to do in these situations is try to learn from the experience. Maybe we had come across as a bit arrogant. Or, more likely, the other agent either knew or had figured out that the mother was the decision-maker and had made his pitch more directly to her. If we had done our homework more thoroughly or asked more of the right questions, maybe we would have focused more on the mother as well—and who knows how it might have turned out. We recruited the Virginia coach, and Tom Collins recruited Ralph's mother. Whether we needed to be more thorough or ask more of the right questions or come across as more likable—or all three—there was plenty to learn from the experience.

Rule #8: Show No Fear

People can sense fear, and if you're not confident in what you're saying or how you're saying it, the person you're talking with won't be either. One of the most difficult things for some people to do is making the "cold call"—a first impression that callers think will leave them looking desperate. But people need each other to make deals happen. The worst someone can say is no.

About seven or eight years ago I made a cold call to GEICO and asked who their chief marketing officer was. I was referred to Mr. Ted Ward, head of GEICO advertising and sales. I called primarily because GEICO's offices are about a thousand yards across Wisconsin Avenue from our office, and I thought the company might be an excellent sponsor of our Washington Association of Tennis Professionals (ATP) summer tournament, the Legg Mason Tennis Classic. After reaching GEICO, we went over to Ted's office for an informal discussion, and during the next hour the chemistry between us was quite strong and friendly. Ted has a great sense of humor, loves to tell stories, and loves all sports, particularly hockey and college basketball. I tried to push him hard to sponsor our tennis tournament. At first he was reluctant, but then he agreed to buy a private air-conditioned suite for twenty seats during the entire week of the tournament.

Thereafter he liked the experience, and today GEICO is the presenting sponsor of our tournament, which is entitled the "Legg Mason Tennis Classic presented by GEICO," for which they pay a large sum in sponsorship costs each year. Ted was also attracted by the fact that the Washington Tennis & Education Foundation (WTEF), a charitable organization, is our partner in the tournament, and he felt he was doing some good for the local community. The relationship has gone on for seven years, and both parties seem pleased with it. Ted and his wife, Joanne, have become good friends of mine over the years, and occasionally we play golf together or go to a Maryland or Georgetown basketball game. All of this was based on a cold call.

Rule #9: Do Good Work

Your reputation almost always precedes you. While the world of business seems enormous, it is really made up of many smaller circles of dealmakers. Once you ruin your reputation with one company, you can bet that the rest of the industry will hear about it. On the other hand, once you've built a reputation for getting the job done efficiently and fairly, you will no longer have to sell yourself so hard. Your reputation will do the work for you, possibly when your survival depends on it.

Before I sold ProServ to the music, concert, and touring company SFX, I had always owned 100 percent of my company and had always financed it myself. But around 1996 I somehow let the overhead get out of hand. In twenty-seven years I had never missed a single payroll, but now I had three hundred employees operating in thirteen different offices and was spending millions annually in overhead costs.

I had reached a financial crisis, and the list of options had gotten very short. Basically, the choice was to fire a group of people immediately, or borrow money. I wanted an instant investor, but I couldn't shop the company around because my competition would immediately smell blood and begin to raid our client list. I was looking for a cash infusion, and given the time constraints and the need for confidentiality, I had to find someone who had complete trust in me and had the resources I needed. I decided to speak with Robert Louis-Dreyfus. Robert was the former chairman of Saatchi & Saatchi, which at the time was the biggest advertising agency in the world but was about to implode when Robert was hired to keep things from falling apart. He did a brilliant job. As a result, he was made the proverbial offer he couldn't refuse by Adidas, which had taken a hit after Horst Dassler's death. If Robert could turn Adidas around, which he did, he would be given an equity stake in the company as a strong incentive.

I did not know Robert at all when he took over at Adidas, but I had had an almost thirty-year relationship with the company, going back to Arthur Ashe and Stan Smith and on up through Ivan Lendl and Stefan Edberg, so I had a lot of credibility with Adidas from the outset.

I really got to know Robert when Carole and I were invited to his fiftieth birthday party, which took place in St. Petersburg, Russia, his wife's original home. He had flown in about 150 of us on a private jet and hosted us for the weekend in the grandest hotel in St. Petersburg.

Robert is a very charismatic and likable businessman. More important, I was impressed with his decisiveness. You never got a "let me think about it" from Robert. He was a brilliant decision-maker and would give you an answer right away.

Robert is also a member of the renowned Dreyfus family, which is among the richest and most powerful in Europe (television actress Julia Louis-Dreyfus is his niece), so if I was going to have one shot at keeping my company functioning well, he was a pretty good candidate.

I saw Robert at the French Open that year and said, "We've negotiated a lot of contracts together in a short amount of time, but I want to talk to you about investing with me personally." Rather than throwing me out of the Adidas hospitality tent, he set up a lunch with me for the next day.

That night I had my daughter Kristina type up a one-page offer sheet. Robert would be my first and only investment partner, but there would be no due diligence, no lawyers, and a closing within thirty days! Not your normal investment procedure.

The next day at lunch I handed him the one-page document, which he read through maybe twice in about three minutes. Then he said, "Okay, I want to do this."

He asked only two questions: Was anyone currently suing me, or ProServ, and would I indemnify him against any potential lawsuits? Since there weren't any current lawsuits, I was happy to tell him no and that I would indemnify him. We shook hands; we had a deal. Less than thirty days later he wrote me a seven-figure check that helped to save my company.

To this day I know that if I had a reputation for being greedy or less than honest, Robert wouldn't have written me that check. Robert also believed in me and in my company. He had witnessed our success over the years and didn't think that it was going to change overnight.

Rule #10: Do Good Works

Some of my best business contacts have grown out of charitable endeavors. But just as with turning business associates into friends, you can't be a fake when it comes to charity. With the celebrity bracelet craze of a few years ago, you probably already know that a lot of famous and influential people run in charity circles. Charities are definitely a networking opportunity, but it is important to get involved with charities that you feel strongly about, where you can devote time and not just money.

One charity to which I've contributed in a major way also became one of my most reliable revenue sources. Nearly forty years ago I started the tennis tournament that is now called the Legg Mason Tennis Classic, in Washington, D.C. The tournament raises money for charity and has garnered about $15 million for children in Washington. In 1972, I gave the tournament sanction to the WTEF, but I continue to run it for them. When I gave it away, however, I stipulated that we would be partners in the event. This would give us exclusive involvement in revenue generation and would in essence prohibit competing companies from gaining a foothold. In the last several years the tournament has grown in popularity, and as of 2009 it is one of the top twenty tournaments in the world.

2

GET NOTICED

In the sports law course I teach at the University of Virginia School of Law, students often ask me how to start their career in the business of sports. Sometimes they are frustrated that even though they'll soon have a law degree, they still feel shut out from the industry. How do the successful people get where they are? What's the difference between them and me?

I always tell them that their education is important—certainly the people who understand the business are going to be more successful. But another part is necessary to get that Air Jordan in the door: dogged pursuit.

Be Relentless

Don't wait for a job to come to you. Go after it with persistence. Start at the bottom of the totem pole—but with the top agencies. When my students ask how they can show their passion, I tell them to write to every one of the top agencies or law firms with sports departments and ask for any kind of work experience. If one of those places offers an unpaid internship, they should jump on it immediately. If they get turned down, they should apply again the next year—but this time with an even better résumé.

This relentlessness also works in the classroom. While many of my students complain about how hard their chosen field is, I always have one or two students who accept it and show their tireless work ethic, enthusiasm, and people skills right from the beginning. When this type of student comes along, I call my contacts at law firms and agencies and ask if they have any room for a new employee.

Nothing is as impressive or effective as persistence.

Get an Asset

Once you have your foot in the door, it is important to take stock of your assets. If you were to mention that you worked for ProServ or any of the other top agencies, a potential client would listen to you even if you were not the senior partner. Similarly, if you're at a boutique agency but have a big-name client, that major player is your asset when it comes to signing other top athletes. Your client list will also be important if you ever decide to leave your agency to start your own.

I had been the non-playing captain of the undefeated U.S. Davis Cup team in 1968 and 1969, and my best players were Arthur Ashe and Stan Smith. I have always said that the greatest thing about the Davis Cup is that you play and compete as a team in what is otherwise an individual sport. When you travel together to different countries as a team, you bond very quickly. It is inevitable, considering the amount of time you spend together.

At the time, I had no hidden agenda or master plan. Stan, Arthur, and I were just friends. I was working for Bobby Kennedy and was starting to build a successful career for myself. The furthest thing from my mind was starting a sports representation business. In fact, I had taken Arthur to meet with an agent, Mark McCormack, in the hopes that Arthur would hire him. Mark was the founder of the sports management firm International Management Group (IMG), and at that time he was the only game in town. A couple of years earlier he had begun representing what was then known as the Big Three of golf: Arnold Palmer, Gary Player, and Jack Nicklaus. That was the beginning of the sports management, marketing, and representation business. Before Mark, professional athletes received salaries or tournament winnings and maybe some personal appearance fees, and that was pretty much it.

But Arthur turned Mark down—not once, not twice, but three

times—because he didn't feel comfortable with him and found him somewhat "aloof." After our third breakfast meeting, we were riding back in a cab, and Arthur, who was now frustrated about this, said, "Donald, why don't *you* represent me?" He added, "If you would do it, I know Stan would join us." Those two great players were all I needed to start my company, Professional Services Incorporated, which I later shortened to ProServ. I was lucky and the timing couldn't have been better, as "Open Tennis" (the professional game) had begun just the year before, in 1968.

Show, Don't Tell

Whenever there is an option to show rather than tell, show always wins out. That's why ad agencies present mock-ups and architects sell models. Clients need to be able to experience what you want to sell them before you've even sold it.

To that end I'm convinced that if a picture is worth a thousand words, an experience is worth a thousand pictures. I am a great believer in looking for any chance to *show* rather than *tell* when trying to close a deal. And once you set your mind to it, there are more opportunities to do this than you might imagine.

If you've ever watched Wimbledon on TV, you may have noticed a prominently displayed Rolex clock as part of the main scoreboard. What is interesting about that is the fact that Rolex doesn't even make clocks; it makes watches.

That deal wasn't made by me; it was made by Mark McCormack back in the early 1980s. But Mark once told me the story of how the Rolex clock at Wimbledon came to be.

André Heiniger, chairman of Rolex, was against associating Rolex with sports in any way. One day, Mark convinced André to attend Wimbledon and arranged to have him sit in the Royal Box. It was a beautiful day, and they had watched a great match from the best seats in the house. Before the next match came on the court, Heiniger stood up and made a sweeping gesture with his arm that took in the entire scene. "Now this," he said, "is Rolex." And that's how the Rolex clock was born.

Of course, no matter how much planning and creativity goes into a potential deal, you can't get your way all the time. I once had what I thought was going to be a similar experience in New York that turned out to have a completely different ending.

In 1998, when ProServ became a part of SFX, I moved my New York offices to 42nd Street and Broadway, directly across from the Ford Center for the Performing Arts, to which SFX owned the naming rights. Ford's contract, which had been a terrible deal, was about to expire. SFX considered me the "naming rights expert" because of the deals I had brokered for the Staples Center and FedExField, and they asked me to find a new company to put its name up in the bright lights of Broadway.

The problem was twofold: (1) the Ford Center was not a sports stadium, and (2) it was difficult, if not impossible, to get a company to buy the naming rights when another company—Ford—had already been there.

I worked very hard to make this deal. We came up with a fantastic visual presentation, and we were able to give it to an impressive list of companies, including MCI, Stevens, AIG, Virgin, Staples, UPS, and Atlantic Trust, but with absolutely no luck.

Meanwhile, I had gone over to take a tour of the theater, which was spectacular—magnificent interiors, three stages, and a host of private rooms that a corporate sponsor could use for all sorts of occasions.

Finally, we were able to generate some interest from a company called Altria. Altria was the new corporate name for Philip Morris, and they were looking to get exposure for their new name. They were impressed with our presentations, but I knew that if I was going to close this deal, I had to persuade the key decision-makers to tour the building itself—to see and feel what kind of place would be associated with their brand name. Amazingly, I got Steve Parrish, who was senior vice president of corporate communications, to agree to do just that.

We were on our way to the theater—I remember it was a Friday afternoon—when all the lights in New York City went out. It was a citywide power outage. When we got to the theater, it was pitch-black. I convinced Steve to wait for a while, hoping the lights of the city would turn back on. They didn't, and our tour was canceled.

The end of the story is that I was never able to get Steve and his group to come back again, and as a result we never made the deal. I am convinced to this day that if we hadn't lost our opportunity to *show* and not just *tell*, the Ford Center would be known today as the Altria Theater for the Performing Arts.

I suppose I should add one clarification: Whenever you get the opportunity, be sure to show rather than tell—but first make sure you can turn the lights on.

Use Shock Value

Before you get a tattoo or bleach your hair, let me qualify that heading. You have to be really confident in your ability to connect with people before you try to make a splash. If you haven't made friends and gotten your foot in the door, you'll probably make the wrong impression. If you're going to say or do something out of the ordinary, it has to make sense. It can't be random or irrelevant. So forget the tattoo and put the hair bleach down. That said, if the situation calls for it, I'm not above making a grand or theatrical gesture or saying something that's a little inappropriate in order to make sure I have everyone's attention.

Many years ago we represented the first high school basketball player to ever jump directly to the pros, Moses Malone. Later it would become an accepted practice (until they changed the rules) for basketball prodigies such as Kobe Bryant and Kevin Garnett to join the NBA straight out of high school, but when Moses decided to go pro, it was very controversial and front-page news throughout the country.

Moses had been offered a contract by the Utah Stars of the old American Basketball Association. It was one of the worst contracts I had ever read. It was a four-year contract with *twelve* additional one-year contracts at Utah's option, potentially a sixteen-year contract for the best high school basketball player in the country.

I had been brought in by Lefty Driesell, coach of the University of Maryland, who had his own ulterior motives. He hoped that by talking Moses and his mother out of signing the pro contract, Moses would end up going to Maryland. I said to Lefty, "I am a totally neutral third party. I am not here on behalf of you or Maryland or anyone else. I am here simply to give my best advice to Moses."

As it turned out, it almost didn't matter. Moses and his mother were staying in a motel in Arlington, Virginia, and when I was brought upstairs to meet him, I encountered the shyest individual I have ever come across. Almost seven feet tall and all kneecaps and elbows, he couldn't bring himself to look at me, although he did limply shake my hand.

I started explaining why I felt the contract was unfair, and after a few minutes I realized I wasn't getting anywhere. He was so uncomfortable and nervous that he wasn't hearing a word I said. A change of approach was needed. I stopped mid-sentence, paused for a moment, and then said, "Moses, have you ever heard of slavery?" His head shot up immediately, and he stared at me intently. "Because," I said, "if you sign this contract, that's like virtual slavery. It could be for the next sixteen years of your life, and I've never seen a contract like this one."

Finally, I had his attention. It was a risky comment to make, but if I hadn't made it, I think someone would have talked him into signing with Utah—and that would have been a disaster for his career.

Don't Sue

A lot of flamboyant agents and lawyers like to draw attention to themselves by suing at the drop of a hat. In today's lawsuit-crazed culture, it seems like a fast way to make a buck, stir up controversy, and build a reputation as the kind of no-nonsense negotiator who can't be pushed around. But in the business world, none of this actually works.

First, it is important to realize that it's generally not in your financial interest to sue. Today you can be assured that a good lawyer will charge a few hundred thousand dollars to see if you even have a clear-cut case. Add that to thousands more for the trial, and you may end up losing even if you win.

Plus, being involved in a lawsuit will take a major emotional toll on both you and your company. Lawsuits aren't glamorous. They are costly and stressful, and instead of making you look tough, they can indicate to the world that you don't understand your business. For example, companies go bankrupt every day. If you have a long-term deal with a company that is folding and can no longer pay the athlete, you have the option to sue or settle out of court. Unless the company is making some kind of ridiculously low settlement offer on a huge deal and won't budge, don't sue.

ProServ and I have done thousands of deals, yet we have rarely sued or been sued.

One of the few people we did sue is tennis star Ivan Lendl. Our contract with all our clients clearly states that we are entitled to our share of ongoing income for any deals we negotiate and finalize, even those completed after the representation agreement has expired. When Ivan resigned as a client, he told us he was not going to pay us our commission on any currently existing contracts, which amounted to several million dollars. So we sued. As it turned out, we settled shortly before the trial for the entire amount that we had estimated Ivan owed us.

In this case, the math was clear-cut: It was going to cost low six figures to collect seven figures. Additionally, Ivan had given us reason to sue, which was that he had absolutely no reason to deny us our percentage. This wasn't a situation where he had gone bankrupt or we had made some terrible deals for him that ruined his image. He had no case, and we had a strong one, which is a rarity in the business world.

3

BUILD TRUST

The class I teach at the University of Virginia Law School is mostly case law—antitrust as it relates to sports and contracts—and the students have obviously signed up because they are entertaining the possibility of getting into some part of the sports industry. On the first day of class I tell them, "If you remember nothing else from this course other than two words, then I will feel I've done my job. Those two words are 'relationships' and 'trust.' To be successful in this business, or in any business for that matter, build relationships that develop trust. Everything else is just noise."

What Is Trust?

But what is trust exactly? It is honesty and integrity, of course, but it's also *doing what you say you are going to do*. If you say you are going to call someone, make the call. If you say you are going to write a letter, write the letter. What I have noticed over the years is that people in corporations are far less likely to do what they say they are going to do or do it in a timely manner than entrepreneurs and people who have their own businesses. Entrepreneurs can't afford *not* to get back to people. Trust is having people take you at your word.

It is also being fair-minded and being able to see beyond your own self-interest. For instance, I could tell you which college basketball coaches over the years had their players' trust and which ones did not. I've been involved in situations where two of the finest coaches ever, Mike Krzyzewski of Duke and Dean Smith of North Carolina, actually encouraged certain players to leave school early rather than complete their eligibility, because, based on that year's draft, it was in the players' best interests.

Finally, it is about leveling with someone, telling it like it is. This is about honesty and telling the person what you really think. It's watching out for the person's best interest. When we sign a new player, I tell that player, "I'm not a manager who's going to try to stroke you. I'm not one of your buddies who is always going to try to figure out what you want to hear. I'm going to tell you what I think is best, and sometimes you aren't going to like it. But if I don't tell you the truth, then you shouldn't be paying me."

You Can't Fake It

There are three facts about trust that every negotiator should heed: (1) you can't fake honesty—even the best liars will get caught eventually; (2) you start to build trust—or destroy it—from the moment you meet someone; (3) trust is relative. I used to think someone either trusted you completely or didn't, but as it turns out, even the most decent and well-meaning people may not be *as trustworthy* as you if they don't bother to answer every question with complete respect and complete honesty.

I learned this lesson with our football client, former New York Jets quarterback Boomer Esiason. He had been approached by more than one hundred agents, and with the help of his coach at Maryland and his father, he had narrowed his choice down to five candidates, including us, to meet with personally.

We had been told that his dad would do most of the talking, so this time we did our homework on the whole family and were prepared to address our remarks primarily to him. But once we walked into the coach's office, Boomer said, "I have an exam tomorrow, so if you don't mind, I'm going to tape your answers to my questions and listen to them later." About an hour later he said, "Thanks very much. Now I have to go study."

It was a very strange experience, because there was very little interaction, and Boomer, because he was simply taping a Q&A, was impossible to read. When we got outside, I said to my colleague, "Boy, did we blow that, and I'm not even sure why."

But I was wrong. Boomer did choose us, and one of the first things I asked him later was what the taping had been all about.

"I asked everyone the same nineteen questions," he said. "I'd get in bed at night and listen to each group talk, and I could tell almost immediately just from their voices and how they answered the questions who was being straightforward and who was being evasive—who the phonies were. When I asked about fee structure, for instance, you were the only one who gave me a straight answer. Everyone else started talking about how they were such great negotiators and marketers. That's why I chose you." (Not surprisingly, Boomer has gone on to have a great post-football career as a broadcaster, commentator, and talk show host.)

You Can't Replace It

The penalty for contributing to a dishonest environment can be very high. If you are open to bribery, for example, it won't be long before *you'll* end up doing the bribing to get clients. The cost of a deal is one thing—sometimes it requires an investment—but circumventing the rules or the law to get your way is a slippery slope that will earn you a reputation as a sleazy negotiator.

Ironically, it was honesty with Boomer Esiason that got me into representing football clients, but it was also honesty that got me out of it forever. Shortly after we signed Boomer, we decided we needed to make more of an organized push into professional football, and practically overnight we hired four people, including two MBAs, to open a separate football division. But we quickly discovered that before they had made the pro team, these recruits had obligated themselves to so many hangers-on, second cousins, neighborhood buddies, and seedy alumni who saw them as their meal ticket that it was all but impossible to unravel the entangling alliances they had agreed to.

It seemed as if every time we reached an understanding, a new agent would suddenly appear and lay claim to our client. There was one incident where one of our football agents had sewn up the top prospect out of USC and was meeting with him at his home the following morning to sign the representation agreement. When he arrived, there were two new Mercedeses sitting in the driveway. Our guy did not have to bother to go inside to figure out what had happened.

Sadly, this type of thing occurred all too frequently, and ultimately we decided that if we stayed in collegiate football, our reputation would suffer. After just six months we shut down our football department at ProServ.

Although our desire for integrity got us out of a lucrative industry, I am sure that if we had compromised our reputation by buying expensive cars to woo potential clients, we would have lost the confidence of other client athletes as well as coaches, who recommend us because they trust us. It is much more advantageous to have someone's trust than to try to buy their loyalty; valuable cars and the sports agents who go with them can be easily replaced. Trust, on the other hand, is an invaluable commodity that you can create from scratch. And it can be passed on—it is contagious.

I have been in two situations where the trust passed on to

YOUR REPUTATION IS YOUR BOND

Marvin McIntyre

McIntyre is the managing director of wealth management at Citi Smith Barney. Currently, MyIntyre is ranked by Barron's *as the number one advisor in Washington, D.C., and the number three advisor in the country.*

I believe that one of the most important elements of deal-making is to only deal with someone who will respect you in the morning. Making a deal with someone you do not instantly trust lowers the possibility of ultimate satisfaction with the transaction. In addition, if you can get humor and lightness into the conversation, you may reduce the tension and allow more productive dialogue.

When negotiating with Legg Mason for permission to turn a hedge fund (something that had never been done at our firm), I went through the normal channels but avoided CEO Chip Mason because I knew that he might want plausible deniability if it didn't work. Upper management didn't want to tell me no, probably because they were afraid that I would hold my breath. So they sent me to the head of compliance, their designated bad cop. When I walked into his office, he introduced me to two other lawyers from the firm. My comment was, "Wow, I didn't know I was supposed to bring lawyers. The good news is that with all of this intellectual firepower we should be able to get this done quickly."

As a final gambit, the compliance head, who was formerly with the company Alex Brown, said, "We had a similar situation with an advisor like you at Alex Brown, and we turned him down."

I smiled and said, "I don't believe there is an advisor like

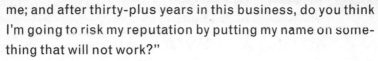

me; and after thirty-plus years in this business, do you think I'm going to risk my reputation by putting my name on something that will not work?"

We made the deal. ■

us was anything but implicit. In fact, it was so direct that it immediately led to major business opportunities for our company. One was a speech that Arthur Ashe gave at a luncheon for the Woman's National Democratic Club in Washington, D.C. The first sentence out of his mouth was, "I'm especially pleased to have here today the two people I would trust with my life. One is my father. The other is my friend and lawyer Donald Dell." Two days later a woman who had attended the luncheon called me on the phone and asked for a copy of Arthur's speech. She turned out to be the mother of Notre Dame basketball star Collis Jones, who became our very first basketball client.

The other example involved the most intense client competition I have ever been part of. It was for the representation of the fourteen-year-old tennis phenom Tracy Austin (at age sixteen, the youngest player ever to win the U.S. Open). Tracy lived in Southern California and had grown up playing at the Jack Kramer Tennis Club, so I called my great friend Jack and asked him to come with me to meet the family, which he was happy to do. Before I could open my mouth, Jack said to Mrs. Austin, "If I had a daughter who was a great tennis player, the only person I would ever want to represent her is Donald." From that point on it was just a matter of not blowing it.

Sports can be a very ugly business, which often ended up working to our advantage. The more players we signed, the more our reputation for honesty and integrity grew—until it had its own self-fulfilling momentum. Our reputation preceded us to such an extent that it became our main recruiting tool.

Get It Up Front

When you are dealing with someone you don't trust, the first rule is don't deal with that person at all. But if you absolutely must deal with the person, get everything in writing and get it up front.

Tennis is often thought of as a squeaky-clean sport, but in many ways it can also be just a more elitist version of boxing. Along with the *mano a mano* competition, there are the entourages, the hangers-on, and the sleazy promoters. I think this is true because both boxing and tennis are global sports, and in other countries these sports are often not as well governed as they are in the United States. This therefore leaves room for a fringe element.

One promoter we dealt with in Hong Kong would pay big guarantees to have certain marquee players show up for the promoter's tournaments or exhibitions. This is strictly against the rules in the major tournaments but an accepted practice in the smaller events. The problem was that sometimes he would pay and sometimes he wouldn't. And sometimes he would cancel the entire tournament at the last minute.

Under normal circumstances you would have to ask yourself: Why would you deal with a guy like this? Life is too short. But in this particular case he also happened to control television rights to sporting events, and not just in Hong Kong but in almost all of Asia—sixteen different countries. Essentially, we couldn't afford not to deal with him.

Whenever he was on the phone, someone in our office would yell, "Get it up front!" So for us he became Mr. Get-It-Up-Front. When you get it up front, it eliminates the guesswork.

Losing Trust

The truth about trust is that once it is lost, it is almost always gone forever. In negotiating, where business contacts become friends and friends are sometimes business contacts, the loss of trust is often perceived as a betrayal, which is a very powerful emotion that is hard to reverse.

For example, I once had a 50/50 partnership with a very good friend in a clay court tennis tournament in France that took place one week before the French Open, which is also on clay. The idea of the tournament was that it would give the players who were used to hard courts and grass the opportunity to practice on clay.

The first two years we lost money on the tournament, primarily because we didn't have an overall—or "title"—sponsor. The third year my friend came to me and offered to buy me out. I thought that was a bit strange, and I asked him if he had found a title sponsor for the next year's tournament. But when he said no, I trusted that he was telling me the truth because he was a friend.

Of course, he did have a title sponsor all lined up, a second-rate watch company that later went out of business and stiffed him on their contract. He then tried to renege on our buyout agreement, but I felt so betrayed that it was one of those rare times where I threatened to take someone to court. We ended up getting all our money, but it cost me a friendship and killed a very promising tennis tournament.

The guy who bought me out had been a friend before he was a business associate, and that may have been what blinded me. Generally, we tend to put more trust in our friends than in a business associate turned friend. My advice is to try your hardest to treat everyone the same. If something seems suspicious (why would anyone want to buy out a tournament that's losing money?), it probably is—even if the deal is with a friend.

Gaining It Back

As I said, it is nearly impossible to gain back someone's trust once you've lost it. But it can't hurt to try, and the best chance you have is discussing the issue openly. Don't pretend that it never happened. That will just make the other party feel more betrayed. Without being offensive or argumentative, be very direct and say, "It's obvious you've lost trust in me. I'm going to get it back."

Don't ask how to get it back. It is your job to figure that out, and it is a very personal issue. For some people it might include inviting them to a tennis match or to dinner to show that you still want them in your business circle. For others it may be handling their needs immediately and in person, no matter what the cost. But the number one rule about losing someone's trust is: *Don't.* Don't get in situations where you know someone will lose faith in you, because chances are, that will be the end of your relationship.

When FedEx and the Washington Redskins were negotiating the naming rights to the team's stadium, the Redskins' owner, Dan Snyder, hired me to do his negotiating because he thought FedEx planned to do the same. In the end, though, I was paid to be a neutral arbitrator because of my good reputation.

After I took the job, I thought I had finalized the agreement. I received a call from Mike Glen, the number two executive at FedEx (who may be Fred Smith's successor) that made my hair stand on end. Mike said he had been looking at the terms of the agreement, particularly the length of the obligation, and felt that FedEx needed an escape clause. He wanted an option to terminate the deal after thirteen years.

"But that's not the deal," I said. "That's like cutting the guarantee in half. If I take that back to Dan Snyder, he is going to cancel the deal—period."

"Well," Mike said, "we can't agree to a contract that goes out twenty-seven years." I argued that I had done this deal directly with Fred Smith, but he said, "If you want to get this deal done, you'll get us that option to terminate."

I fretted for a couple of hours and then decided that I had no choice but to call Fred Smith directly. When I finally did, his assistant said, "This is good timing, Donald. He is in there with Mike Glen and our general counsel, Alex Masterson. Let me put you right through." When Fred picked up, he said, "Hey, Donald. I'm here with Mike and Alex. Let me put you on speakerphone."

I panicked and almost hung up, but instead I said, "Fred, your lawyers are insisting on an option to terminate after thirteen years—"

Before I could finish my thought, Fred interrupted. "But that's not what we agreed to. Our deal is a flat fee for twenty-seven years."

"Thanks, Fred," I said. "That's all I needed to know."

About an hour later I received a call from Mike Glen. "I'm very angry over this," he said.

"Listen," I said. "I just protected you by blaming this whole misunderstanding on the lawyers. I kept you completely out of it."

"You went over my head," he said, "and I'm going to remember that for a long time."

People do have long memories, particularly when they feel you have crossed them in some way. Here I thought I had done the right thing by putting myself in the middle as the mediator, beholden to neither side, and I ended up losing the trust of Fred Smith's likely successor at FedEx.

On the plus side I figure I have a few years before Fred Smith steps down, which is my window for figuring out some way to make amends with Mike Glen.

4

WIN BEFORE YOU BEGIN

Tennis legend Bjorn Borg was known for having ice water in his veins. (His nickname was "The Iceman.") The greater the pressure, the better he seemed to play. We never represented Bjorn, but I once asked him how he managed to remain so cool under pressure.

"Actually," he said, "I get terrified. If it's my serve, sometimes I think I'm not even going to be able to toss the ball up in the air. My senses are so on edge I can hear someone in the stands coughing in the top row. But I know that if I can just put the ball in play, my strokes are going to take over and I'll be fine."

One of the most common questions asked of the players is how they manage to stay calm when the matches get tense. Their answer is always the same as Borg's: "Preparation and practice, practice, practice until muscle memory takes over."

I first learned this lesson in 1968 when I took over as captain of a not very good U.S. Davis Cup team. The first thing I did was to hire a tough taskmaster coach, Dennis Ralston. I then demanded an additional two weeks from the players before each round for nothing but practice and playing one another. This way I knew for certain that we would be match-tough going into the tournament. Finally, I hired a trainer, Gene O'Conner, whom we called "Everready" because, from a fitness standpoint, he'd always have us ready to play. That doesn't sound as important now because today almost every player has a personal trainer, but then it was revolutionary.

As a result, I took a long-shot team to the championship, and we won. The United States hadn't won a Davis Cup in many years, but our team defended the title again in 1969, beating Romania (Ilie Nastase and Ion Tiriac) 5-0 in the Challenge Round.

Of course, "muscle memory" isn't going to help you a whole lot in the business world. But preparation—not only knowing your stuff but knowing more than the other guy—will help you win before you even begin.

Take the Time to Learn What Others Won't

The more relevant facts and figures you have memorized before you go into a negotiating room, the better off you are. If you have more information than the other person, you're at a certain advantage. I honestly believe that negotiations are often won and lost based on the knowledge and preparation that someone brings to the table. It is not just numbers. The best negotiators know a company's history, how similar deals turned out so and everything about the person they're negotiating with.

The most successful I've ever seen at this was Robert Sillerman, the founder and CEO of SFX. (He is now CEO of CKX, Inc., which owns the rights to Muhammad Ali, *American Idol,* and Elvis Presley.) SFX owned or controlled every major music venue in the United States and monopolized rock-and-roll tours as a result. Sillerman sold at such a premium to the radio giant Clear Channel that they have yet to figure out how to make it pay for itself.

I sat in on several negotiations with Sillerman, but my first-hand experience of being on the other side was when he bought my company, ProServ. He was so prepared and threw out so many facts and figures that he appeared to know a surprising amount about my privately held company. My head was spinning within a half hour of sitting down with him. His briefcase seemed to contain an infuriating amount of information.

The cumulative result of that type of preparation is that he ended up conducting both sides of the negotiation: "We'd like to do that, but this is what would keep us from doing it. On the other hand, we could do that, but here's the problem . . ."

Don't get me wrong. I made a nice sale of my company. But I was so surprised by his facts and documents that to this day I have a lingering suspicion I might have gotten more.

SEE IT FROM THE OTHER SIDE

Stan Kasten

Kasten, now president of the Washington Nationals, was the youngest general manager ever in the NBA when he accepted that job for the Atlanta Hawks at age twenty-seven. He has also been the president of the Atlanta Braves.

I've often said *preparation* is the most important aspect to making a deal. Know *all* the pertinent rules. All the economic factors. All the personalities. All the histories. And perhaps most important, know as well as you possibly can what your counterparts or adversaries are *really* trying to accomplish. You may not be able to achieve something that works well for both sides, but your chances will be much greater if you have a clear understanding of what the other side wants. And, of course, if you *can* satisfy your counterpart's needs while still achieving your own goals, making a deal should be easy. Needless to say, you can't accomplish this without knowing everything you can as early in the process as possible.

In June 1990, as president of the Atlanta Braves, I was in the market for a new GM. Naturally, the media listed dozens of names for me. Those lists consisted mostly of people who were then unemployed (or who had never done the job before). There were some fine names, but I wanted to find someone who was so good that he actually had a job at the time. I took three months identifying the top people who would fit the profile I needed to make us a championship organization. I then pursued my top choice with an approach that I thought would compel him to leave his existing safe and comfortable position to come to Atlanta and help build an organization. I needed to convince him that this was a unique opportunity and worth the risk. I also needed a lot of luck, and many other things had to fall into place. But by the end of the season I was able to announce that we would be hiring my first choice, John Schuerholz, away from the Kansas City Royals, which is arguably the greatest hire I ever made. ∎

Assume There's Something You Don't Know

I can't tell you how many times I arrived prepared for a negotiation, only to have someone or something come up that upset or changed the deal I thought I was doing. The only way to protect yourself 100 percent against this situation is to assume there is something you don't know. This advice will not only keep your mind up to speed with the deal and force you to consider the other party's motivations, but it will also keep your ego in check.

The second part of this advice is to never stop learning. Knowledge, like trust, is relative—relative to what the other people in the room know. That is why you need to be proactive about building on the knowledge you already have. Once your learning curve flattens out, there is a greater chance that the "something you don't know" factor will catch up with you.

Recently, during a basketball negotiation, I had a moment

where I was surprised by how much I knew. I think this is probably true of anyone who has been doing the same thing for any length of time. You accumulate knowledge whether you are trying to or not, and it's the best kind of knowledge because it is practical, firsthand knowledge.

But it wasn't always this way. I remember the first time I negotiated an NBA basketball contract. I had negotiated plenty of other contracts, so I figured an NBA contract would be similar. Wrong. In this negotiation the team's general manager said he was offering my client more salary than anyone else on the team and showed me the contracts of several of his best players to prove it. At the time I thought the deal was a winner.

Of course, I learned later that a basketball player's annual salary is only part of his financial package. How much of the money is deferred? What about the "loans" that will be forgiven and other forms of compensation? What was the signing bonus, the reporting bonus, the various incentive bonuses, and so on down the line? I hadn't thought that there would be aspects of dealmaking unique to basketball, and I wasn't prepared for what I didn't know.

Compare that story to the negotiations we had after we had a little more knowledge, specifically once the salary cap came in. The NBA owners by definition are a successful group. Otherwise, they could never have bought an NBA team. But when pitted against one another, they were such profligate spenders that in 1983 they negotiated a clause to protect them from themselves called "the salary cap," a historical first that forever changed the game. The only problem initially was that the salary cap was so complicated (and still is), almost no one understood it, including the owners!

I used to tell people that the head of our basketball division was the only human being who actually understood the salary cap. Shortly after the salary cap came in, we had a negotiation with a team that shall remain nameless. Both the owner and the GM were telling us that they couldn't offer what we were asking for one of our players because it would put them over the salary cap, which it might have. But my colleague had gone to extraordinary lengths to learn what he could about the salary cap rules and said something like "I don't see the problem. Once you trade so-and-so to Portland and then trade the new player to the Lakers plus a player to be named later, which you have already said you are going to do anyway, you'll not only have room to pay our player, but you'll get to keep your mid-level exception."

Over the years this became our MO. Invariably we would understand the cap and all its complexities better than most of the GMs we negotiated with, which gave us an advantage. Because we didn't stop learning and adapted with the change in policies, we were more prepared to deal with surprises along the way.

Today, inside knowledge of the players' salaries is less important than it once was. With the help of the Players Association we now know what every basketball player is paid and how the compensation packages have been structured. We no longer have to take the owner's "word" about whether they are really over the salary cap or not. Thanks to the Information Age we know almost as much about a team's finances as they do. It eliminates a lot of the guesswork and enhances our negotiating position. Learning to navigate the NBA contract language was another instance where we used a new tool to build on our knowledge.

Never Try to Fake It

When you are suddenly faced with a problem you can't solve, don't pretend you know the answer. It is this type of egotistical response that often gets negotiators into trouble, because they usually come across as more ignorant than if they admitted they didn't know the answer. It seems that anytime I have not done my homework or tried to fake it or came across as knowing more than I actually knew, it always lessened my effectiveness.

For a couple of years we represented Pudge Rodriguez, the best catcher in baseball. We thought he was worth more than his team was willing to pay, so we went to arbitration. In baseball arbitration the owner names one price, the player names another, and both present their best case. Then the arbitrator decides which one it's going to be. I went up against a young lawyer named Frank Casey Jr. (I had once worked for his father in Washington), and he slaughtered me. In a basketball negotiation I can come at you several different ways, but this was my first baseball arbitration, and other than comparable salaries, I didn't know how to establish value. Casey, on the other hand, threw out a bunch of numbers: batting averages with runners in scoring position with two outs, percentage of runners thrown out at third base, and so on. I still felt that Pudge was the most valuable catcher in baseball, but if I had been the arbitrator, even I would have voted against me. I knew we had lost before the arbitration decision came back.

A year later the Texas Rangers offered Pudge a very good long-term deal, but he wanted to go to arbitration again. I had dinner with him in New York to try to talk him out of it, but he had already made up his mind and was adamant. I even made a joke about how he was going to fire us if we lost again, and he said, "Oh, no. I'd never do that."

I walked into the arbitration hearing, and who arrives for the Rangers but Frank Casey Jr. We got our butts kicked again, but this time I discovered that baseball arbitration was all Frank Casey Jr. did! He said he worked on twenty-five to thirty arbitration cases a year for the Major League Baseball owners. Simply put, I was not as experienced in arbitration cases as Casey Jr., but I tried to fake it—twice—and lost twice.

About a week later, spring training started, and Pudge had a new agent.

One of my most embarrassing not-knowing-my-stuff moments took place so long ago that it should have faded from memory, but it was such a silly mistake that it refuses to go away.

Satellite technology was still relatively new at the time, and we were trying to sell the broadcast rights for a series of European clay court tennis tournaments to PBS here in the United

States. Why PBS? Because we had already sold them a surprisingly successful series of U.S. clay court tournaments for Monday night tennis (featuring Bud Collins and me as the commentators), and it seemed a logical way to build on that success.

I was well into my pitch when a PBS executive stopped me and said, "Donald, I'm sorry, but we could never do this. Just the costs to PBS for broadcasting from Europe would be prohibitively expensive."

"I think you're wrong about what this would cost," I said. "With the *spoons* we could bring in the whole package from Europe for about the same amount as the current series is costing you."

Everyone in the room, including my head of television, Dennis Spencer, got these curious looks on their faces. Finally, after a painfully long moment of silence, Dennis said, "I think what Donald means is dishes—satellite dishes—not spoons."

Fortunately, everybody in the room knew me well enough to laugh about it. To this day I have trouble understanding new technology, but from a lesson learned long ago I know better than to try to pass myself off as an expert on anything involving technology!

Have a Backup Plan

No matter how much you prepare or how good you are under pressure, you can't get your way all the time. If you do, I can assure you that you've made some bad deals. Not all deals will go through—that's the nature of negotiating. But the difference between a mediocre businessperson and an expert is that an expert always has something in his or her back pocket. Once that backup plan becomes the forerunner, it becomes your goal to make it into an even better deal than the original one.

A well-researched backup plan also gives you leverage. If you think you have only one shot at making a deal happen, you'll take anything you can get. But if you have developed other options, it will give you flexibility.

While writing this book, one major deal of mine has been falling apart before my eyes. Not long ago I obtained a terrific six-year deal with a major shoe company for a basketball player client of mine. But in October 2008 the company discovered that it wasn't doing as well as expected and might need to get out of basketball altogether. My client's deal is still good as I write this book, but I know that won't be the case for long. Soon my client will have the option to sue (not likely) or settle for an offer that the shoe company will make. At that point he'll be without a contract and looking for me to make him a new deal.

Because I maintain my relationships, I am aware of the impending fallout and have been working on a backup plan before my client is without a shoe and apparel contract. I also know through networking that Kevin Plank, the CEO of Under Armour, is looking to broaden his business to include basketball shoes and apparel. If the shoe company informs the player that it can't pay his contract, I'll be waiting, hopefully with an even better contract in my pocket.

5

SIZE UP PERSONALITIES

When you are dealing with monstrous corporations, it's easy not to take individual personalities into account. But companies don't make deals, people do. "Reading people" is an important concept because it includes everything about them, not just the words they are speaking. Tone, body language, and how these match or mismatch with what you already know about them all come into play when reading people.

Negotiate Backwards

Reading people—understanding their thought processes and their emotional makeup—that is what gives you the ability to predict the future.

I call it "negotiating backwards." Go in with a clear picture of where you want to ultimately be. (As they say, if you don't know where you're going, you're never going to get there.) Then, based on your ability to read the person involved, say and do whatever is necessary to get you where you want to go.

The best I've ever seen at this was my mentor, Sargent Shriver, whom I worked for when he was the head of the Office of Economic Opportunity (OEO) under Lyndon Johnson. He would say, "Donald, when you go up on the Hill today, Senator So-and-So is going to say this. Then Senator So-and-So is going to say that. Here is what I want you to say."

It was uncanny. He would give me both sides of the conversation, and usually, like magic, we would end up with the funds we were looking for.

Jack Kramer, Wimbledon and U.S. champion, was also a great reader of people and had an ability to predict the future based on his understanding of the personalities involved. It was Jack Kramer in his role as president of the Association of Tennis Professionals (ATP) who led the successful boycott of Wimbledon in 1973.

The International Tennis Federation (ITF) had gone to the chairman of Wimbledon and persuaded him not to accept the entry of a talented Yugoslavian player by the name of Niki Pilic, which was totally against the ATP rules.

I was Jack's general counsel for the ATP at the time, and he and I went to Wimbledon and told them that if the ITF did not reinstate Pilic, seventy-eight ATP players were going to boycott the tournament. Primarily because tennis is largely an individual sport, tennis players are notoriously fickle and self-centered, so I thought this move was incredibly risky. I wasn't at all sure that the players would be willing to go through with the boycott.

But Jack had read the players correctly. He understood that they were tired of getting pushed around by the powers-that-be at ITF and Wimbledon. The players could see that this was a much bigger issue than their own individual self-interest, and all seventy-eight signed the boycott letter. And they went through with it. An almost unknown player by the name of Jan Kodes won Wimbledon that year. As you can imagine, this was the number one sport story in the world at the time and the number one story in England. It was a very gutsy move, and it was based totally on Jack's ability to sense the mood of the players and their determination not to get pushed around by officialdom.

Don't Trust the Résumé

First things first: Don't ever judge someone—whether it is a potential employee or someone with whom you might be negotiating—by a piece of paper or by his position. Some of the most successful people in the world are some of the shadiest. What you get in person is a much more legitimate evaluation: People spend years honing their résumés, but their true character comes out when you put them on the spot. If you sense that someone is not completely honest, I don't care how many deals that person has done or what schools he or she attended, the person is not worth your time.

It is very rare that I completely misread someone, but when I do, it is often because I am judging him or her from reputation instead of personal experience. That was the case with venture capitalist and Texas Rangers owner Tom Hicks. Hicks is probably best known for doing the worst deal financially in baseball history: the $250 million–plus deal for Alex Rodriguez, which should have been a warning sign right there. (The Red Sox trading Babe Ruth to the Yankees is the worst deal overall.)

I met Hicks through Roberto Mueller, the founder of the Pony shoe company, and that gave me some level of comfort. Hicks had started a sports cable channel, PSN, which was like the ESPN of South America. This was a few years ago when I was still employed by Clear Channel. I had sold Roberto the South American cable rights to the U.S. Open tennis for a lot of money, $20 million over four years. The first year they broadcast 108 hours, and the United States Tennis Association (USTA) was delighted—until it came time to collect the first payment. The contract had been signed and the product delivered, so I felt it was obviously some misunderstanding that could easily be straightened out. Certainly no one was going to not pay after broadcasting 108 hours. (How much proof of a deal could you possibly have?) But PSN kept hemming and hawing to the point where I was starting to feel that perhaps I was being stonewalled.

The next thing I heard was that Hicks had fired all the executives of the company and closed it down! Now I could not reach anyone on the phone, much less have my calls returned.

Finally I felt I had to go to Lowry Mays, who was the CEO of Clear Channel. "Lowry," I said, "I have a big problem. There's this man in Texas who owes the USTA a lot of money, and we may have to sue. His name is Tom Hicks."

"Oh my God, Donald," Lowry said. "Tom Hicks's investment company is the single largest shareholder of Clear Channel! He has $2.4 billion invested in this company!"

Needless to say, this was making a lot of people uncomfortable. The next thing I knew, Clear Channel held a board meeting and voted *not* to sue Tom Hicks's company. Meanwhile, the USTA was pressing me to make good on the money. I was caught between a rock and a hard place.

Thankfully, I received a call from Randall Mays, Lowry's son and the COO of Clear Channel, who said, "Let's go to Dallas and visit Tom Hicks."

When we got to Hicks's office, Randall brought up the TV money issue, and Hicks said, "I'm losing my ass down there. The USTA has to get in line with all the other creditors."

To Randall's credit he said, "Tom, if you don't take care of this, my dad might have to ask you to leave the board."

"All right," Hicks said grudgingly. "Donald," he said to me, "call my assistant and get it straightened out," and then he changed the subject.

The bottom line: We never got a dime. Tom Hicks, CEO of a major venture capital firm and one of the wealthiest people in the country, simply did not pay the USTA and SFX because he knew he could get away with it.

THINK LONG-TERM

Jorge Paulo Lemann

Lemann is a former world-class tennis player and a founder of the Brazilian investment banking firm Banco Garantia. He also owned AmBev, a Brazilian brewing company that merged with Interbrew of Belgium in 2004 to form the world's largest beer company, InBev, which recently acquired Anheuser-Busch in the United States.

A great deal is one that is long-lasting and self-sustaining. Many deals can be very good for the short term but have little long-term perspective. Instead of being a quick fix, our recent combination of AmBev and Interbrew to create InBev has an agreement of twenty years between the shareholders.

My biggest success in business was the discovery some forty years ago that by attracting excellent people to work with me and giving them a chance to grow, I would go much further than I would by myself. ■

Styles Make Negotiations

Each of us has an individual style that we bring to the dealmaking table. Everybody is different, but after years of dealmaking I've noticed patterns among people and realize that many negotiators fall into one of several categories. Here's my list of broad personality types based on some of the most well-known people who illustrate them:

- David Stern, commissioner of the NBA. David is the most able marketer of all the commissioners. He is also a smiling assassin. You think he's the nicest guy in the world, but then you walk two blocks and your head falls off.

- Donald Trump. He is outstanding at understanding how his reputation precedes him. You are so prepared for the worst that, when he comes across as a decent guy, he has you eating out of his hand. Donald Trump also has more chutzpah than almost anybody I've ever met. I barely knew "The Donald" when one day he called me and said, "I saw Gabriela Sabatini play, and I want to take her out. I want you to set it up for me." I said no, but I heard that later he did find a way to get Gabby's number (he is also relentless) and did ask her out. She refused.

- Bob Kraft, owner of the New England Patriots. Bob is a very warm guy. He comes across as a kind of sleepy-eyed, absentminded professor. He asks random questions almost as if he's confused. In reality, though, he's about six steps ahead of you. Smart as hell.

- Bill Clinton. I've obviously never negotiated with him, but if I had, he would have killed me, because Bill Clinton is the best "people person" I have ever met. He has a natural talent for it that you notice right away. At one point my daughters worked for Hillary Clinton, and a few months later Carole and I found ourselves in the receiving line at a White House dinner honoring Eunice Shriver, founder of the Special Olympics. As we approached the head of the line, I was trying to think of what I wanted to say in the ten to twelve seconds we would have in front of the president. But before I could open my mouth, he said to Carole, "How are [your two daughters] Alexandra and Kristina?" I was stunned.

- Robert Kennedy. Bobby Kennedy *wasn't* a natural people person. There was no small talk with Bobby, mostly because he was shy, and that took some getting used to. But he could also be very confrontational. He had a mental toughness about him that made him very decisive, a great decision-maker and leader.

Dealing with Oddballs

The key to dealing with oddballs is never to underestimate them and believe that they have earned every good deal the same way you have. Their success is no accident, and to diminish or ignore it is to proceed at your own peril.

If I were to define oddball behavior as eccentricity, then I would say that Phil Knight, founder and CEO of Nike, would certainly qualify. Phil would show up at the most important business meetings wearing jeans, a ratty T-shirt, and old sneakers. Also, he was convinced that Nike was superior in every possible way, which sometimes made it difficult to have a rational conversation with him.

But the main thing I got to know about Phil Knight is that he is as sharp and as smart as they come. I have found this to be true of many so-called oddballs, particularly if they are successful. In fact, often their success is a function of their eccentricity: They have found a different or unusual way of looking at things. They are often the doers, the risk takers.

Generally I believe these people know who they are, and it is best to acknowledge their "eccentricity" in some sort of nonthreatening or humorous way.

Arguably the most notoriously difficult person to deal with in tennis (although less so now than earlier in his career) is Richard Williams, father of Venus and Serena Williams. I first met Richard when I went out to visit Venus and Serena, who were, respectively, fifteen and fourteen. Richard, who isn't much of a tennis player himself, was the girls' only coach. They were rumored to be prodigies, but no one knew for sure until Venus was given a wild card for one of the professional women's tournaments at age fifteen and won several matches.

Serena had yet to prove herself, and she was still fairly young (though not by tennis standards; Tracy Austin was sixteen when she won the U.S. Open), so Richard pushed to have them both represented as a package. Richard made his pitch and then said, "Now I'm going to leave you with my accountant and my lawyer to work things out." As soon as he was out of the room, the lawyer said that Richard first wanted a $350,000 payment "for being their father," which, as best as I could determine, was really some sort of finder's fee.

I'm not often speechless, but at that moment, I was. Finally I said to his accountant, "Look, suppose I gave you some of my top clients to represent as their accountant, but first you had to pay me a fee of $350,000. How would you feel about that?"

"Well, you know," the lawyer said, "IMG is coming down here tomorrow."

"Great!" I said. "Tell them I offered Richard $500,000. They may match it." And that was the last thing I said before leaving without offering Richard a penny.

Of course, we ended up not representing Venus and Serena, and until recently IMG represented both of them. To this day I don't know if they paid Richard his fee.

Richard is a rogue, a rascal—and a genius. I think he has been great for the game of tennis, which still suffers organizationally from too many stuffed shirts or empty suits. When I saw Richard recently at Wimbledon, I yelled at him in front of a crowd of people, "Richard—why aren't you in jail yet?" He laughed and said, "I'll get back to you."

If you try to engage Richard as you would a normal person, he'll say something like "Yeah. Great to see you," and then brush you off. But if you come at him as if you know he's a little off center, then you'll end up having a good conversation. I find that I like him in spite of myself.

Dealing with the Overly Cautious

In the business world it seems strange that some people are not eager to make a deal, but when you're dealing with large sums of money, a certain amount of caution is always involved. The problem is that you can come across people who are so cautious that they fail to follow through, or they hem and haw over a deal so long that it gets stale. There are different types of non-dealmakers, but I can safely say that if you use humor, are firm and direct about what you need, and identify their motivations, you'll have an easier time dealing with them.

Sometimes if you say something in a lighthearted way with just the right tone, you can get away with murder. Right now I'm dealing with someone who is very high up at one of the major apparel companies. I like him personally, but he is so ready to say no to our ideas that I don't think he even hears what we're saying.

When I called him recently, he picked up the phone himself. Before I even identified myself, I said, "Oh, is this the guy who says no before he says hello?" I think I embarrassed him a little bit, but he really couldn't show it. I can't say that he's now our best customer, but he definitely hears us out and gives our ideas reasonable consideration—and sometimes even says yes.

But when the person you're trying to make the deal with seems indecisive or hems and haws, that's when it is best to counter immediately and directly. You must show the person that you're not interested in dragging out the deal and are not amused at watching him drag his feet. Whatever you do, don't get sucked into his time line of the deal if you think it will hurt you.

I was recently in a meeting that was a follow-up to a particularly contentious negotiation. I had given our differences a lot of thought and felt I had come up with a solution that would solve the impasse and have something to satisfy everyone. The only problem was that I knew the meeting would be filled with notorious second-guessers, and even if everybody agreed it was a good solution, they would spend the rest of the meeting talking themselves out of it.

So I went right at them. As soon as everyone was seated I said, "I have given this a lot of thought, and I think I have come up with a compromise that addresses all of your concerns. My only problem is that once I put this out on the table, you're going to spend the rest of the meeting taking potshots at it. So I think I'll just save it until the end."

Obviously, if I had come up with a way to break the impasse, no one wanted me to save it until the end of the meeting, so someone said, "No, Donald. If it's as good as you think it is, then I promise you that we won't second-guess it."

Now they had painted themselves into a corner. If they liked my proposal, they pretty much had to accept it as it was, without going back and forth. And that's exactly what happened.

In that instance I felt I could be particularly straightforward without coming off as insulting, because I was addressing a roomful of people and no one person could feel singled out. When you are dealing with an individual, however, things can be a little more delicate. In these situations I recommend being firm and direct by creating deadlines, real or imagined. Tell them you have to get the deal done in this fiscal year or you're going to have a meeting with so-and-so, who's going to want to know if this is complete.

That is how I have dealt with Arlen Kantarian, the former CEO of Pro Tennis for the USTA, who really takes his time—too much time—on every deal. I respect Arlen, but he can be infuriating. Just when I think I've gotten a deal nailed down, he'll say, "So what about this?" or "I need to give it some more thought" or "Why don't you speak to so-and-so?" or "I may need board approval."

I have been a consultant to the USTA and, by extension, the U.S. Open television for a number of years. Most of my back-and-forth with Arlen has been over television rights, but recently my own consulting contract had come up for renewal. I had just helped Arlen and Pierce O'Neil, the USTA chief business officer, finalize the biggest deal for cable rights in the U.S. Open's history with ESPN, in a six-year contract for over $110 million after months and months of negotiating, so the timing for me could not have been better.

As a reward, Arlen said he was going to factor a "success fee" for the ESPN deal into my new contract, but after months of negotiating, on those few occasions when I could actually get him to address the subject, we made no progress. When it comes to hemming and hawing, Arlen is absolutely the best I've ever encountered.

In the process, either intentionally or otherwise, he ironically gave himself a tremendous amount of leverage. Pretty soon Arlen's own contract with the USTA was going to expire, and if for some reason it was not renewed, all the goodwill I had accumulated with Arlen for the ESPN deal would be walking out the door with him. If there was a new USTA pro tennis director, my own negotiations would be starting from scratch. So much for any "success fee."

Finally, Arlen had his lawyer write a draft of their offer. I was stunned. It was far worse in both length and consulting fees than my current contract or even the previous one. It was disappointing, almost insulting. After spending about a half second looking at just the numbers, I got back to the USTA's lawyer and said, "Tell Arlen I'm not even reading that piece of nonsense." It was a tough thing to do. I was essentially saying to them, "Come up with something a lot better than this—and do it quickly—or you are going to lose me."

But I also had some leverage of my own in the form of a deadline: Arlen's contract renewal issues cut both ways. I knew a lot of people on the USTA's board, and he was going to need my support. For his own self-interest he almost *had* to get my deal done. Second, we had just finished a successful negotiation with ESPN, and we came out of it with a new working relationship with them. If I didn't get rehired, then Arlen and the USTA would be losing some of that goodwill.

After we had exchanged some nasty emails ("I don't like your attitude," "My job isn't to make you happy"), he finally said to me, to avoid a bigger confrontation, "I'm going to the Australian Open in two days, so I'm turning this over to my USTA lawyer. She has full authority to make the deal." After that, we reached agreement quickly, with a deal that was fair and good for both sides. (Ironically, Arlen, of his own volition, resigned nine months later.)

At some point you'll probably be confronted with a person who doesn't seem to find value in the same things as everybody else or is just generally hard to read. For these people, discover their motivations and values. If you find that their motivations are completely selfish, you should probably get out of the deal.

That may be what I should have done with my most difficult client of all time, tennis player Jimmy Connors. I've dealt with any number of people who were hard to read, but in the case of Jimmy, he and his mother, Gloria, served as each other's alter egos.

Individually, they were okay. All you had to know about Jimmy was that he was very much like his on-court personality: defiant, stubborn, and relentless. You really had to be a contrarian with Jimmy: Figure out what was in his best interest and then suggest just the opposite. Jimmy was often stubborn just for the sake of being stubborn, but once you figured this out, he was fairly easy to manage.

To give you just one example of Jimmy's perverse nature, after he retired, he really wanted to do color commentary for one of the networks, and in 1991 I managed to negotiate a sweetheart four-year deal with NBC Sports. Tennis was included in the Olympics in 1988, the first time since 1921, so Jimmy's contract included a clause that said he would also commentate on tennis for the Olympics in Barcelona for NBC.

The first year went great, but when the Olympic year came around, Jimmy refused to go. "It's ten days," he said, "and maybe they'll do a total of three hours of tennis. It's just not worth my time."

When I told Ken Schanzer, president of NBC Sports, he was dumbfounded. "I don't get it," he said. "Almost anyone else would be thrilled to spend time at all the other events, hanging out and just having a good time. But I can tell you this right now, if he doesn't go, we are terminating his contract."

And that's what happened. Jimmy still refused, and they terminated his contract. As a result, NBC was desperate to find a replacement, and in the eleventh hour they found someone else: John McEnroe. And that was the beginning of McEnroe's illustrious broadcasting career.

After a while I realized that the defiant Jimmy and his domineering mother, who called me regularly, were different but had the same motivation: It was all about Jimmy getting what Jimmy wanted, no matter who got put out in the process.

Once, we organized a TV commercial shoot for Sony with Jimmy in L.A., where he didn't bother to show up. Sony told us they would never deal with him again even if he were "the last athlete on earth." When I told Jimmy, he just shrugged.

All you need to know about how Jimmy and Gloria "worked" together was how he came to us originally and how he left.

Jimmy had previously been represented by IMG. The weekend before he left, Jimmy and his agent at IMG, Bob Kain, had chartered a plane and made a prearranged trip to five different tennis clubs in Florida looking for a club with which to affiliate as their "touring pro." On the preceding Friday, Gloria had written a note to Bob but made sure it wasn't delivered until Monday morning. The note said that IMG's services had been terminated. Bob was stunned and felt used.

Jimmy was with us for eight years, which was remarkable when you factor in the difficulties involved in representing him. One day I was driving home when I received a call from Gloria Connors. Not taking her call or saying that you will call her back weren't options with Gloria, no matter how trivial you knew the subject might be. "Wait a minute, Gloria," I said. "Give me a moment to pull over. Okay, what's up?"

Gloria started out as if it were going to be a typical phone call about her problems with our arrangements for Jimmy. "Donald, I have three things we need to talk about. One, I don't like Jimmy's schedule in Japan. Someone has committed him to way too many personal appearances, and I want you to cut them back. Two, the new shoes that just came in from Converse are too narrow, and they're squeezing Jimmy's feet. Converse is fixing the problem, but until we get the new shipment, I want you to get someone to cut slits in the sides of all the shoes he will be wearing in Japan. Three, we're changing agents."

With that, I said, "Let's discuss number three first!" But that was pretty much it. There was a bit of back-and-forth discussion, but that was the end of our representation.

As to Jimmy, I still have mixed feelings. On the one hand, he was one of the most difficult clients we ever represented. On the other hand, he was the greatest show and ticket seller in the history of tennis. He never gave up, he fought like crazy, and he knew how to electrify a crowd.

6

EVALUATE THE
SITUATION

The primary distinction between this chapter and the previous
one is that reading people is about understanding the personalities in the room—their quirks, their temperaments, their likes
and dislikes, their negotiating styles. (One person can lose his
temper, and it means absolutely nothing; another person can
lose his temper, and it means the end of the deal.) Reading the
situation is more about how the personalities interact with one
another, the nature of the discussions, and the nature of the deal
itself. It is very much about accurately taking the temperature of
the room or plugging into the vibe.

Pay Attention

As stressed before, research on specific personality types is key. You must know everything you can about the people you're dealing with before walking into a negotiating room, because you won't have time to get to know them during the negotiation. Instead, you should be focused on the here and now—the specific atmosphere this specific combination of people is creating. This takes a lot of focus, so pay attention to everything. If you ever get bored because you feel you know everything, you're not doing your job. Once in the negotiating room, you should be gauging everyone's interactions with one another. You'll be shocked at all the hidden messages you'll discover.

When Jimmy Connors was still my client, I had invited him, his wife, Patti, and their children to stay in our guesthouse while Jimmy played in the Washington, D.C., tournament. (This is the one I had founded as a charity event; it is now known as the Legg Mason Tennis Classic.) At the time Jimmy was ranked number one in the world, and the idea was to give him some privacy and a place to relax and spend some quiet time with his family.

But I also wanted to use this time as an opportunity to nail down his schedule for the coming year. The Sunday before the tournament started, I invited several people from the office who were involved in various aspects of Jimmy's career out to the house to discuss the time that Jimmy needed for sponsors, for personal appearances, and so on.

As the men from my office started pitching Jimmy, he began to fidget quietly in his chair. This was not like him at all. Jimmy was usually talkative, outspoken, and direct. Because I was tuned in to the interaction, I sensed almost immediately that this meeting had been a big mistake. First, I knew the one thing Jimmy hated more than anything was being pinned down, and that's more or less what our people were trying to do. Second, we were not as prepared as we should have been. We started arguing with one another about how best to spend Jimmy's time without even consulting him. And we were doing this in front of Jimmy!

It didn't take a genius to read this particular situation. My reasoning had been to get him in a relaxed frame of mind and that would be when to discuss his schedule. Instead it had the opposite effect. In fact, I had provided the people who were pulling him in different directions. I could sense that Jimmy was getting increasingly agitated, but potentially more damaging, I could sense that he felt he was being taken advantage of.

Perhaps it wouldn't have been so bad if we had shown more preparation, but the way things were going, I canceled the meeting almost as soon as it had begun. (This didn't particularly endear me to some of my key associates, who had come out to my home in rural Maryland on a Sunday afternoon for business.)

As soon as everyone had left, I immediately apologized to Jimmy, and while he accepted my apology, I could tell he was feeling exactly the way I had feared he would—as if he had been set up. Needless to say, that was the last time we discussed Jimmy's schedule for the remainder of that week and for quite a few weeks to come. At least I had properly read the situation, and it didn't cost us a very important relationship, which I think it very well may have otherwise.

Many times you can sense a bad vibe when someone gets uncharacteristically quiet, like with Jimmy Connors. Whenever there is a negative atmosphere in a business meeting, it's best to acknowledge it privately. With Jimmy I had created the bad environment, but that is not always the case. Even when you are not at fault, bringing up a negative ordeal with clients or associates makes them feel comforted. When you show people your concern, they feel that someone understands them and knows why they are upset. They are also reassured that you're on their side and on the same page. Ultimately, they are more likely to trust you when you give them evidence that you can relate to their concerns.

One particular time with Michael Jordan I did not create the bad situation, but when I read his mood and acknowledged it, it helped solidify our relationship. One of my assistants and I had arranged to meet Michael for dinner in Chicago after a game to go over a number of issues ranging from a contract renewal to several endorsement opportunities. We sat in the rear of the restaurant, Michael with his back to the patrons so that no one would disturb us. But no sooner had we been handed menus than Michael's teammate Charles Oakley walked in with a beautiful woman, pulled up a couple of chairs, and invited himself to join us.

Oakley is six feet eight, and in real life he looks like a mountain. He was what is known as an "enforcer" on the basketball court and, to some extent, Michael's bodyguard during games. He and Michael were also good friends, so it was not my place to tell Oakley that we had some business to discuss and to bug off.

In any event, Chicago had won the game, and Oakley was clowning around a lot. At first Michael went along, but as the evening wore on, I noticed he was getting very quiet. It was becoming pretty obvious that Oakley wasn't going to take a hint, and Michael was too polite to ask him to leave. I sensed Michael was not very happy that our business dinner had been totally destroyed.

The food finally came and went, and Oakley was just getting warmed up. My assistant and I excused ourselves and said we were headed back to the hotel. Once outside, I said to him, "Michael is really upset. We need to call him as soon as we get back to the hotel." (It's hard to believe there was ever a time before cell phones when you had to "get back to the hotel" in order to call someone.)

As it turned out, I had read the situation correctly: Michael was really upset, and although it obviously wasn't our fault, at the end of the day the onus was on us to make it right. We rescheduled our meeting for breakfast the next morning and covered the issues we needed to cover. It gave us an opportunity to show that we were responsive to his sensitivities and the pressures that he had to live under.

KEEP THE HUMAN TOUCH

Ted Leonsis

Leonsis is vice chairman emeritus of AOL and the owner of the NHL's Washington Capitals.

The best deals have an outcome that can be anticipated and fall into alignment with the spirit of the deal. Always start the negotiation with your expected outcome in mind. Do gut checks along the way. Communicate early and often among senior-level negotiators. Make sure to avoid personal attacks and negativity, and communicate well with the attorneys so they, too, know exactly what you want to get done. Understand both viewpoints. Keep the human touch by being direct, authentic, and empathetic. Communicate a lot after a deal gets done to make sure the deal is the start of a relationship, not the end of a transaction.

One noteworthy strategic deal I made years ago was when I aligned a young company, Google, with AOL. AOL received technology and services from Google; Google received traffic and a percentage of revenues and the glow of the AOL brand. AOL had made an investment for equity and received warrants. The deal has generated multiple billions of dollars for AOL and served customers well. It has also helped Google create more than $100 billion in value for the company and become the number one new media brand in the world—a win-win situation for both AOL and Google. ∎

Don't Fall in Love with Your Own Voice

Listen more than you talk. Making deals is not about showing off, it is about listening, observing, and trying to pick up some clues that will help you anticipate what is going to happen next. You never learn anything at all when you are talking, and, of course, when you are not talking, it is also harder to put your foot in your mouth.

During my tenure at SFX, a young man in our office procured the naming rights to the Jones Beach Theater on Long Island, New York, and had even managed to get a modest offer from an apparel company. He came to me because he had heard that I knew some of the senior people at Nautica, which he thought would be a perfect fit for Jones Beach, not to mention a competitive bidder. Nautica's chairman, Harvey Sanders, is a good friend of mine, so I was more than happy to set up a meeting.

Harvey is a real straight shooter with a low tolerance for BS, so I don't think he would have taken the meeting unless he was very serious, and I actually thought we had a good chance of making a deal—until I heard from the young associate that his boss in Los Angeles, who also worked with us at SFX, insisted on attending this meeting as well. His boss was actually someone I had hired years ago to work for me at ProServ. He was a very aggressive, pushy type, and I never really warmed to him.

We met with Harvey and two of his marketing men, and the deal was pretty much done. Nautica offered substantially more than the other company, but it was a take-it-or-leave-it offer. Harvey did not want to negotiate, and he did not want to get into a bidding war. He said that if there was to be a bidding war, "we will withdraw our offer," but there would be no hard feelings. Harvey could not have been clearer or more specific. I thought it was a no-brainer.

But then my associate's boss began his pitch. "You know how much we want to do this deal with you, Mr. Sanders," he said, "but right now you aren't even in the same ballpark. As I've already told your marketing director—perhaps he didn't share this information with you—if you want to see Nautica's banners flying over Jones Beach Theater, you're going to have to up your offer by at least a million."

He must have gone on for another ten minutes—what a great deal it was, all the benefits, blah, blah, blah. I was so embarrassed, I almost got up and left.

I looked over at Harvey. He wasn't saying anything, but from the look on his face, I could tell he was furious. Anyone with half a brain could see that he couldn't stand this hard sell—this bullying—and he couldn't stand the guy who was doing it.

As soon as they left, I called Harvey's office and left a message. When he called me back, I said, "Harvey, I didn't see that coming. I am so sorry."

He said, "Donald, I appreciate the call, but there's absolutely no way we are doing this deal—ever." Of course, we ended up going with the other company for a lot less money.

This is obviously an extreme example, but I've seen versions of this happen all the time: Someone is so completely in love with his own voice that he misses the most obvious cues and fails to take the correct temperature of the room.

It's Your Job to Keep It Pleasant

Deals often fall apart because of the tension that builds up in the room. Consider it your job to defuse any tension and keep things pleasant. Once you take this stance, you will seem more mature—above all the silly fights and embarrassing displays of anger—and I guarantee that people will respect you more and be more willing to make a deal with you.

One of the most tense negotiations I've ever had was over the renewal of Michael Jordan's second shoe deal with Nike. You would think that this would be a slam dunk, but the original deal had been so spectacularly successful for Michael that Nike was determined not to renew under the same terms. (It had obviously been spectacularly successful for Nike as well, but for the moment that was being conveniently forgotten.) Things finally got so tense that it came down to a phone call between me and Nike's legendary founder, Phil Knight. Phil told me straight out, "We're not renewing Jordan's deal under the same terms, and that's final." Nike is often very difficult to deal with, but Phil is a no-nonsense guy, so when he said this, I totally believed him.

I backed off. I said, "Phil, if we can't agree on Michael's deal, then let's agree on something else. Let's agree to meet in Chicago [which was about halfway between Nike and ProServ] and get a hotel suite. You bring your lawyer, and I'll bring one of my associates. And whether it takes ten hours or ten days, we won't leave that hotel room until we have a deal."

Phil agreed on the spot. As I mentioned, Phil and I had previously bonded over a couple of bottles of wine at the Italian

Open, and I thought that if I could get the two of us in the room face-to-face, we would figure out a way to get the deal done.

We flew in on the same day and took a "negotiating suite" at the Hyatt Regency in Chicago. We had been going back and forth for about three hours when Phil suddenly said, "That's it. I'm going home."

"Wait a minute," I said. "We specifically agreed we would not leave this room until we worked this thing out."

"Well, I made a mistake. I just can't deal with all this arguing."

He did have a point. The discussions had become very contentious and seemed to be getting worse. Suddenly I realized what the problem was. If the two of us couldn't agree, how were four of us going to agree?

I pulled a few twenties out of my pocket, turned to the lawyers, and said, "I have an idea. I would like you two to go have a leisurely dinner and don't come back until midnight."

Once Phil and I were alone, we knocked out the outline of a deal in about four hours, and the lawyers memorialized it the next morning.

You aren't always in a position to kick everyone else out of the room as I did, but you *can* say that you need a few minutes to talk privately with your counterpart. Sometimes just a couple of minutes in private with the other side can move things along at a much faster pace than when everyone is in the room.

With Phil I had also imposed a deadline—midnight—without its really seeming that way. I think we both would have been a little bit embarrassed if we hadn't negotiated a deal by the time our colleagues returned.

Look at the Big Picture

The biggest problem with accurately reading situations is to understand that you are part of the problem. In other words, since you are inside the situation yourself, it is hard to look at it purely objectively. Sometimes it can be really helpful to take a moment to step back and look at the big picture. How are you progressing in terms of reaching your objectives? What is standing in the way? What is your part in it? What can you do about it?

Even though this anecdote isn't strictly about business, I want to tell a story that illustrates this point of looking past the minutiae at the larger picture. In fact, I want to tell it because, first, many of the lessons in this book can and should be applied to personal as well as professional matters, and, second, it has never been told before. Had it come out when it took place, twenty-five years ago, it would have made front-page headlines all over the world and probably gotten Bill Talbert and me ostracized from tennis. It is the story of how I helped to salvage the finals of the 1983 U.S. Open in a match between Ivan Lendl and Jimmy Connors.

During practice on the day before the finals, Connors ended up with a giant blood blister between two of his toes. It was like a stone bruise—really big and really painful. On the morning of the match Jimmy tried to practice, but not only couldn't he run, he could barely walk. Shortly thereafter I got a call from Jimmy's mother, Gloria, who said, "Jimbo can't play. Default him. He's out."

When I heard this, I thought: "Jimmy's thirty-two years old. He may never get this opportunity again. CBS and the USTA are going to go ballistic (not to mention the tennis public) if the U.S. Open finals doesn't happen." The growth of tennis had started to plateau, and I could see this non-final really hurting the game. Once I stepped back and considered all the options, I felt I had to do something.

Through a friend I got in touch with the New York Jets' team trainer, told him the situation, and asked him if there was anything he could do to relieve the pain. "Sure," he said. "I could shoot him up with Xylocaine," which is like a souped-up version of novocaine. This would mean Jimmy wouldn't be able to feel the toes that were in pain.

So I asked my Jets trainer friend, "How would you like to attend the finals of the U.S. Open?"

Now I had to persuade Jimmy to go along with the plan. I walked into the locker room. There were about five people surrounding Jimmy—including his wife, Patti, his bodyguard, and one of our agents—but fortunately, not his mother. I said, "Give me a few minutes alone with Jimmy."

Once we were alone, I said, "What's the story?"

"I can't play," he said. "I've got to default. Even if I could limp around, I'd rather not play than have Lendl beat me."

"What if we could fix your foot so you could play?" I said, and then I told him about the trainer for the Jets.

He was still unsure, so I said, "Let's be honest here, Jimmy. You're thirty-two years old, and you have a shot at winning your fifth Open. I know you think you'll be back, but we both know there's a good chance you may never get to the finals again."

He said, "Well . . . if you handle my mother . . . "

I said, "I'll get the trainer."

The trainer told us the shot would last about an hour and a half, so I thought, "Damn. I'm going to have to find some way to pull Jimmy off the court in the middle of the match so the doctor can shoot his foot up again."

I then went to the tournament chairman, Bill Talbert, and told him what was going on. "I can't authorize that," he said.

I said, "Well, you have two choices. You can let me fix his foot, or he'll default and you'll have no tournament final."

Talbert said, "I never heard about this."

Under the tournament rules, each player can leave the court once at any time for a bathroom break, so I went to the tournament supervisor and told him, "I'm going to take Connors off the court at some point for a bathroom break. I don't want any interference. I don't want anyone bothering him. I also want the biggest policeman you can find sitting in a chair right out front of that bathroom door. And when Jimmy goes in, I want that cop to block the door so no one can get in there."

He wasn't too happy about this, but Talbert was standing right there, so he nodded.

This was in the old stadium, the Louis Armstrong. One of the bathrooms is located directly across the court, slightly to the left. I told the trainer I'd give him a hand signal when it was time for him to go into the bathroom . . . and hide.

Finally the match started, and I began to wonder, "If this goes more than three hours, we're dead." Jimmy won the first set 6–3 but promptly lost the second set 6–7.

Now the score was 2–1 in the third, and Jimmy had started to limp noticeably. I signaled the trainer.

Jimmy called for a bathroom break and started to walk across the court. Meanwhile, Ivan Lendl, who is very smart and very cagey, was the only one in the stadium who figured it out. He started screaming to the tournament supervisor, "Watch his foot! Don't let anyone touch his foot! Don't let him out of your sight!" But no one paid any attention—or, more likely, the officials decided to ignore him. If they chose somebody to accompany Jimmy into the bathroom, we'd be out of luck.

Connors came back to win the third set and the fourth, and made tennis history by becoming the only man at that time to have won the U.S. Open five times. (Pete Sampras would later repeat the feat.)

Afterward the official doctor for the Open, Dr. Irving Glick, came up to me and said, "Donald, I don't know what you did, and I don't want to know."

I said, "If that's the way you feel, fine. But I can live with what I did."

At the press conference later, the first question to Jimmy was, "Why did you have to leave the court?"

"I had a horrible attack of diarrhea," Jimmy said, and that became the official story that appeared the next day in the *New York Times* and the *Washington Post* and was told on *The Late Show with David Letterman*.

USE OBJECTIVE COMPARISONS

Lowry Mays

Mays is the founder and former CEO of Clear Channel Communications and was inducted into the Radio Hall of Fame in 2004.

The most important aspects of making any deal are having respect for the other party and negotiating with the utmost integrity.

It is very difficult to isolate the best deal we ever made at Clear Channel, but as far as creating a lot of momentum in the early days of the company, a deal that stands out is our acquisition of two Louisville, Kentucky, radio stations. They were the number one and number two stations in their market, and while they were profitable, they did not generate the kind of revenue they should have been generating.

I did an analysis of Cincinnati, Ohio, and Louisville and found that Cincinnati had twice the radio revenue of Louisville even though the cities were about the same size. Since we were dominant in the Louisville market, it simply meant we were underselling our product. While it wasn't easy, we doubled our prices to match Cincinnati's over time, and as a result, doubled our revenue. That cash flow significantly funded the growth of Clear Channel in the early stages. ∎

7

STACK THE DECK

The next three chapters are a kind of trilogy on the use of leverage. This chapter is about how to create an edge for yourself when you don't otherwise have one. The next chapter is sort of a subset of this chapter in that it is specifically limited to the power of words—what you say and how you say it—to get an edge. And the chapter after that is about how to best use the leverage you already have as you go into a deal or the leverage that the other side simply hands you during the course of making the deal.

For many years we competed fiercely against the International Management Group, particularly in tennis. The head of IMG's tennis division at the time was Bob Kain, and recently I asked Bob to address my sports law class at the University of Virginia to talk about his own experiences with recruiting and representing professional tennis players.

I had no idea what Bob was planning to say, but he started out talking about me! "When I first came to IMG," he said, "the question I had to ask myself was how I was going to compete with Donald Dell. He was a former player, and he had been captain of the U.S. Davis Cup team. His company represented the French Open and the U.S. Open, and he knew just about everyone who was anyone in tennis. I was just out of college, and while IMG already had an impressive tennis roster, I felt that I lacked any kind of credibility."

I didn't know where Bob was going with this, but now I was just as curious as my class. "Everywhere I went," he continued, "the players and their families would say, 'Donald Dell promised that he was going to handle me personally.' I finally realized there was no way he could handle all those players himself personally, so I started making a list."

At this point Bob pulled out his wallet, took out a yellowing piece of paper, unfolded it, and held it up for the class to see. I would say it had the names of about forty tennis players on it.

"From that point on," he said, "whenever Donald's name came up, I'd show them this piece of paper and say, 'Look, here's a list of all the players that Dell has promised the same thing, that he would represent them personally, and now he's saying the same thing to you.'"

I was completely stunned. Bob had always been a very effective recruiter, but this was more than twenty-five years ago and I was learning about it for the first time. And technically, Bob was right. I *did* promise all those kids that I would handle them personally—along with one of our younger guys. It always turned out that our younger guys were more available, were much closer to the players' ages, and they had more in common with them. After a couple of months they didn't want to talk to me anyway, which is why I was able to handle so many players "personally" and rarely got any complaints.

But that list became a very effective recruiting tool for Bob. Strategically it was a very smart thing to do and a good example, I believe, of creating an edge for yourself, of stacking the deck in your favor. It is also a form of leverage, but it's the kind you make for yourself as opposed to the kind you already have going, which will be discussed in a later chapter.

First They Have to Like You

My best leverage by far? Perfectly situated courtside boxes at both the U.S. and French Opens. The best way to immediately endear yourself to almost anyone is to do them a personal favor or, better still, a favor for their boss or someone in their immediate family. It's one thing to give someone prime seats at the U.S. Open, but if you are able to include his or her children, it takes it to a whole new level.

One of my more important business relationships is with Ted Ward, the senior vice president of sales and marketing for GEICO, which is a major sponsor of two of my top television properties, the French Open and the Legg Mason Tennis Classic. Ted has absolutely no interest in tennis, but in getting to know him better, I discovered that his wife, Joanne, loves the game and follows it closely. This year I invited Joanne and a friend of hers to Paris and entertained them in my box at the French Open. For Ted the French Open is just a smart media buy, but getting to know him and his wife has not only helped develop more of a personal bond between us but also given me an opportunity to show my appreciation for his loyalty.

Not everyone has tickets to courtside seats at the U.S. Open or Giants tickets on the fifty-yard line. But if it is an important new relationship, it's worth asking yourself, "What do I have to offer this person that he or she would really appreciate?" Maybe it's helping his kid get an internship or putting in a good word at his alma mater. Maybe it's introducing her to someone who could be helpful to her business or her career.

Or maybe it's just lending a sympathetic ear. Recently I called to confirm an appointment, and when I sensed the person on the other end was a little distracted, I asked if everything was okay. He opened up a little , and as it turned out, he had recently received some upsetting news about his health that was really bothering him.

"Listen," I said. "Forget our meeting, but I'm going to come over anyway and we'll just talk"—which is what I did. He was very appreciative, and it helped solidify our relationship. I had been given the opportunity to take what might have been a disaster of a business call and turn it into something much more positive.

Look for Common Ground

Another strategy for establishing a personal relationship with a potential business partner is to look for common ground and then make it about the other person. Because I genuinely like people, this is something of a no-brainer for me; I would much rather learn about someone else and find our common ground than talk about myself. (But even if this were not the case, I would find a way of making it so.) Most people, when properly approached, enjoy being asked to talk about themselves or their children. It naturally breaks down barriers and leads to everyone's being less on guard.

Last year we concluded a deal with ESPN that got quite a bit of publicity; it was for the cable rights to the U.S. Open (for those evening and weekday matches that were not being covered by CBS, which was most of them) for well over $100 million in TV rights fees. I negotiated with a smart, experienced executive, John Skipper, whom I had never met before. We met for the first time for breakfast. I looked for common ground, and immediately detected a Southern accent. I asked him where he had gone to school, and when he said the University of North Carolina, I was able to engage him in a good conversation about my relationship with Dean Smith, about our recruitment of Michael Jordan and other UNC greats, and about my older brother, Peter, who had also played tennis at UNC.

Anyone who overheard our conversation would have said it had nothing to do with dealmaking, when, of course, it had everything to do with dealmaking. It was this conversation that set the foundation for the next six weeks of friendly and productive negotiation and ended in a fair deal for both sides.

Suppose John Skipper had not gone to UNC. Then my hope would have been that he went to school somewhere else where I had a past history. If not, I might have asked him where he grew up or how he got to ESPN. My point is that within four or five questions I can establish common ground with almost anyone—usually it's someone we both know—and then get the person to open up about himself or herself. It sets the right tone for everything that is to follow.

Also, when meeting someone for the first time or when dealing with someone I don't know very well, I make it a point to try to keep things light and, if possible, engage that person's sense of humor. If you make someone laugh, it's almost impossible for the person not to like you. I'm not talking about a laugh-out-loud joke. That can easily backfire. What I am talking about is something that might elicit a smile from the other party as it relates to the conversation.

Recently I called someone I didn't know very well, Tony Ponturo, the former executive vice president of Anheuser-Busch Media, the largest buyer of sports television in America. I immediately launched into how much I loved the Budweiser commercial that features the Dalmatian dog training one of the Clydesdale horses to make the "first team" while the *Rocky* theme plays in the background. Tony told me that as a result of that commercial, which played during the 2008 Super Bowl, Budweiser had been flooded with positive letters and emails from across the country, particularly from animal lovers.

After we had discussed it a little bit more, I finally got to the point. "The reason for my call," I said, "is that I would love to see that horse and that dog at the French Open. I have a great television ad package for you."

Tony chuckled at the time, but after discussing it for a few days with some of his colleagues, he decided to pass. Then he added, "We'll do something together in the future." I would have loved to make a deal, but far from being disappointed, I felt as if, with one lighthearted comment, I had laid the groundwork for something else down the road.

Money Talks

Of course, the most obvious manufactured edge is money—offering more than the other guys. As they say, the golden rule of business is "He who has the gold makes the rules." And while I would like to think that I have now been around long enough to have outgrown even the hint of any remaining naïveté, I am still often surprised at how often it comes down to money.

Obviously, the vast majority of deals I have made were and are based on who was offering the most money, but there have been times when other factors, such as relationships, loyalty, who is going to do the better job, or even who is hungrier, would come into play. For several years Michael Jordan was a spokesperson for Coca-Cola. When his contract came up for renewal, Michael told me he did not want to renew. I was incredulous. "Michael," I said, "I don't understand. They're paying you a lot of money, and they make almost no demands on your time."

"That's the problem. They aren't using me. My endorsement income depends on exposure. The more that I am out there, the more my value goes up. Let's find someone who's going to use me correctly."

And that was how we ended up with Gatorade. Michael understands that the value of the Jordan "brand" is even greater than the money, and this, of course, was long before branding was the only thing companies could talk about.

Now it always seems to be about "how much," with nothing else factored in. It is no coincidence that one of the most famous lines about greed—"Show me the money"—came from a movie about sports agents.

I also know how it feels to be on the short end of the money stick. Over the years the change that most negatively affected our business was when it became acceptable, and even expected, to offer marketing guarantees to the clients you were recruiting. Almost overnight it went from who is going to do the best job to who is going to take the most risk financially in signing a client.

This was one of the ways in which IMG often managed to win a recruiting battle. Mark McCormack, who was once named "the most powerful man in sports" by *Sports Illustrated* and spent two decades at the top of the *Sporting News'* "most powerful" list—had built IMG into an international force. They were more than three times our size, and once guarantees started to come in—in terms of tournament or player fees or marketing dollars—we just couldn't compete. They had all the money in the world to throw around, and we didn't. By comparison we were a mom-and-pop operation, and we had to rely a lot more on guerrilla tactics and building relationships in order to stay in the game.

Another one of IMG's "tricks" when competing for clients was to guarantee more dollars than anyone else for something reasonably small, such as a personal appearance fee, even if the client never knew that IMG often made up the difference out of their pocket. For instance, suppose they were competing for a particular golfer. They would ask him what his agent had been getting him for one-day corporate golf outings. Whatever the number, IMG would say, "We think we can double that," and they would—and would continue to do so once the golfer became a client even if IMG had to make up 100 percent of the difference. It was simply the cost of doing business. It was diabolical, but everybody won—except the other agents—and it was a great way of creating an edge.

Bid 'Em Up

Having an alternative offer in your back pocket gives you another money-related edge. Of course, once you've stacked the deck in this manner, it becomes a question of whether or not you want to reveal your hand—to keep it as your own little secret or to encourage open bidding.

You don't need everyone to want what you are selling. It just takes two. The ultimate way to create leverage for yourself is to start a bidding war, but you have to be very careful about when you do it and how you go about it.

While this seems primarily a question of strategy, what you end up doing often depends on what is acceptable within a particular industry and whether or not there are a number of players of more or less equal strengths. In the book publishing industry, for instance, it is accepted and even standard practice to submit a proposal for a potentially big book to several publishers simultaneously in the hopes of starting an auction. Closer to my own home, there are often open bidding wars in the athletic footwear industry (LeBron James doesn't walk away with a $90 million deal from Nike because they are nice guys; it's because they had to outbid Reebok) and among the television networks—and now many of the cable channels—for the rights to broadcast all the major sports events.

Make 'Em an Offer They Can't Accept

What often prevents you from getting the best deal is that one party, by virtue of a preexisting agreement, has the right of first refusal or the right to match anyone else's offer (which obviously discourages bidding) and thereby the right to extend their agreement. How can you get around this contractual edge? By making them an offer they are unable to accept. This requires an explanation.

NBC now has the network rights to the French Open, but that wasn't always the case. For several years it was broadcast over CBS and probably would continue today had they not been so arrogant. CBS not only had the right to match anyone else's offer but they had the first right of a thirty-day exclusive negotiating period, otherwise known as first negotiation, first refusal (FNFR).

Philippe Chatrier, president of the French Tennis Federation (they owned the French Open, which I represented), loved what NBC had done when broadcasting Wimbledon both in terms of the way it was promoted and the way it was presented. NBC had turned it into "appointment television" ("Breakfast at Wimbledon"), and their ratings had soared. Chatrier wanted the French Open to be on NBC as well, but because CBS had the right to match any offer, it was highly unlikely.

As it turned out, NBC had been thinking along the same lines. They wanted the French Open and were prepared to pay a lot more than CBS to get it. During CBS's exclusive negotiating period, I gave CBS all sorts of warnings, but they fell on deaf ears. After all, they could always match anyone else's offer.

Then NBC did something clever. (In fact, I wish I had thought of it; I have used versions of it since then.) As part of their offer, NBC proposed promoting the French Open and Wimbledon together as a single promotional package in their ads and television spots. Since CBS didn't have Wimbledon, there was no way they could match this offer.

Admittedly, this was a bit borderline, but my client wanted NBC badly and this was his opportunity. Once the head of CBS Sports, Neal Pilson, learned that we were actually going to do this, he called me. As a negotiator he was a steamroller, but this time he said, "Donald, the new president of CBS—my boss—just started. Don't hang me out to dry on this one."

"It's too late," I said. "You had an exclusive negotiating period. Philippe also told me your people went behind my back and called him to negotiate directly. This train has already left the station."

In truth, I did feel terrible about it. It also cost me immensely. CBS refused to deal with us, and I was persona non grata there for almost three years—and this was before cable really took off, so there weren't a whole lot of other options out there for tennis. But my job was to serve the best interests of my client, and if I had to do it over again, I'd do the same thing.

As it turned out, this story had an interesting postscript. CBS sued NBC over this matter, and then they quietly settled the suit without anyone else knowing about it. What I would later learn is that CBS wanted to sign NBC's legendary baseball announcer Vince Scully. So NBC ultimately gave up its rights to Vince Scully in return for CBS's dropping its lawsuit against the French Open.

CREATE YOUR OWN OPPORTUNITIES

Kay Koplovitz

Koplovitz was the first woman to head a television network when she founded USA Networks under the banner of Madison Square Garden Sports in 1977. She also launched the Sci Fi Channel and currently runs her own media advisory and investment firm.

The first Major League Baseball contract ranks high on my list of best deals I've made. It was what you call "making lemonade out of lemons." The year was 1978, and I had just helped launch the first all-sports network, Madison Square Garden Sports (predecessor to USA Networks), and made a deal with George Steinbrenner of the New York Yankees to air their games.

The first Yankees game on MSG was an amazing extra inning affair against their archrivals, the Red Sox. I was thrilled. But the next morning I received a call from the commissioner of baseball, Bowie Kuhn, who told me that I didn't have the right to carry the game. When I explained I had a contract with Steinbrenner, Kuhn told me that only Major League Baseball had the right to sell the games, and if I didn't pull the rest of the Yankees games immediately, he'd get a restraining order to stop me. I told Kuhn I'd call him back.

After consulting my lawyer about the restraining order, I realized I was up against a force I couldn't beat. I whipped up the courage to call Kuhn, and after about ten minutes of trying to persuade him to allow the Yankees to continue on MSG, I had gotten absolutely nowhere. Then I said to Commissioner Kuhn: "I'll trade you."

"I don't know what you're talking about," he said. "Trade me what?"

"The Yankees contract for a contract for Major League Baseball. We'll televise the games of all the teams."

Silence. I waited. Finally, he said, "I'll see you in my office tomorrow morning at nine a.m., Ms. Koplovitz."

And that's how we became the official television network of Major League Baseball. ∎

"We Try Harder"

Sometimes there *are* things that are more important than money. One of the most successful advertising campaigns in history was the Avis "We try harder" campaign. At the time Hertz was by far the number one car rental company in the United States, and Avis was a distant second, but the customers believed that Avis really was trying harder because they had more to gain. That campaign ended up dramatically closing the gap between the two companies.

In a way the Michael Jordan "Air Jordan" deal might never have happened had Nike not convinced us that they were going to try harder. Jordan had worn Converse in college, and at the time Nike was a much smaller company. But they flew Michael out to their headquarters in Oregon, gave him the grand tour, and treated him like royalty (which he almost became). Nike then laid out such an impressive marketing plan that it became their edge—and the rest, as they say, is sports marketing history.

I had something very similar happen last year. Shortly after Joakim Noah announced he was going pro and declared for the NBA draft, I flew to Paris to meet with Antoine Sathicq, the president of Le Coq Sportif, the European apparel and sports marketing company.

I had considered this mostly a courtesy call—Joakim's father and my former client Yannick Noah were on LCS's board—because Joakim really wanted to go with Nike, and Le Coq Sportif wasn't even into basketball and not yet selling in the United States.

I could tell immediately that Antoine was a very smart guy—he was the former head of Adidas in France—and one of the first things he did was take me to his warehouse, where he brought out two pairs of shoes, one a leisure shoe and the other a high-performance basketball shoe. "This is a prototype," Antoine said, "but it has already been tested in the professional leagues in Spain and France and refined several times. We think it is now the best basketball shoe ever made."

Very smart. They had done more than just their homework; they were ready to go, and if it was not going to be with Joakim, it was going to be with someone else. Antoine laid out an equally impressive launch campaign and then made Joakim an offer that was hard to refuse—a substantial guarantee against a royalty on all basketball merchandise, including apparel, with the potential of becoming a part owner of the company.

Now we were interested. On the one hand, we had all the leverage. Le Coq Sportif saw Joakim as their ticket not only into basketball but also into America. On the other hand, Antoine was a very impressive guy, they had a great product, and, most important, they couldn't afford to fail. Antoine had created an edge for himself, and that edge was that success was going to be far more important to them than it could ever be for any of the other established shoe companies. LCS was hungrier.

Now compare that to Nike's effort to "attract" Joakim. As I said, he was very hot to go with Nike, and I knew that Phil Knight was very eager to have him. Nike had signed LeBron James two years earlier, and I got a call from the guy who was his liaison at Nike. He flew to Washington to see me. He was very high on Joakim and said that Nike would do whatever it took to get him. (Apart from his basketball skills, Joakim is also a tremendously appealing personality. He must certainly be the only seven-footer in history to wear a bow tie to the NBA draft.) Then the NBA playoffs began. Cleveland and LeBron were in the playoffs, and for six weeks I could not get this guy to answer emails or return my phone calls.

This was obviously a very strong signal, intended or otherwise, that Joakim wasn't as high on their priority list as we had been led to believe, and I finally got so annoyed that I sent a note to Phil Knight. Immediately, of course, my phone started ringing, first with apologies and then to set up meetings. They wanted to fly Joakim out to see their campus in Portland. Nike is a great company, but they have gotten so big that they're like IBM or Procter & Gamble, where the right hand doesn't always know what the left hand is doing.

In the meantime, Antoine and Le Coq Sportif, in playing out their hand, had given me a great hand to play as well—a very intriguing offer that Nike or Adidas probably couldn't match or beat no matter how badly they wanted Joakim. Normally when I have a good offer, I put it out on the table to see what kind of response it brings, but because I thought it was so unlikely that Nike would or could attempt to beat it, I decided to keep it in my back pocket.

It's a great feeling to go into a meeting where you have nothing to lose and only something to gain. I did not want to come across as cavalier, but after being stood up for six weeks, I wasn't really looking to help them out either. I decided to wait and see what kind of opening offer they would make and let that determine where we would go from there.

Nike flew three people in from Portland for the meeting. LeBron's guy was not among them, so first I had to find out who had the authority to make their offer. It turned out to be this fairly young rep, and I could tell that this was one of his first negotiations because he was visibly nervous.

There was already a lot of tension because of how this meeting had come about, and when I refused to even throw out an offer, the tension got even worse. Then the rep said, "It's Nike's policy to never make the first offer."

"Nonsense," I said. "I've done countless deals with Nike, and you're the first one to ever bring this up." There was this awkward silence in the room because he really didn't know what to do next.

Finally, he said, "We're in the range of around a half million dollars."

I said, "What the hell does that mean?" Now he looked so nervous I almost felt sorry for him, so I added, "You're not even in the same ballpark. We're looking for a royalty and a guarantee of at least twice that much."

Then he got angry and dug in his heels. "That's our offer," he said. "We aren't going above $500,000." I'm pretty sure he had the authority to go higher, but now he had painted himself into a corner. He had let it become about his ego.

From their very first phone call to their final word, Nike had done everything in their power to forfeit any edge (Joakim's number one choice) they had from the beginning. Since I now knew for sure that this wasn't going anywhere, I started playing for the future. I wanted to leave them with the impression that I do not respond well to ultimatums. I waited a couple of beats and then said, "Okay, fine. I respect that. I've got to go now." Then I got up and left.

Gestures Can Speak Volumes

One of the smartest and toughest negotiators I ever knew was Lamar Hunt, the original owner of the Kansas City Chiefs. He was instrumental in combining the American Football League and the National Football League, and the American Football Conference's champion receives the Lamar Hunt Trophy in his honor each year.

He was also the founder of World Championship Tennis

(WCT), which was one of the earlier American tennis circuits in the 1970s. One day we were negotiating over some WCT-related issue—it was so long ago that I can't even remember what it was about—and after the dinner hour came and went, it started to become obvious that this was becoming less about whatever the issues were and more about who was going to outlast the other.

As the evening wore on, I was getting tired and started yawning. I excused myself to go to the bathroom, but my real purpose was to splash some cold water on my face to try to revive myself.

When I returned to my office, Lamar Hunt was on the floor doing push-ups! I threw my hands in the air and said laughingly, "Okay, I give up!" To this day I don't know if he was exercising to keep himself alert or trying to show me that he was just getting started. It really didn't matter, because either way it worked.

Most gestures in a negotiation are obviously less dramatic than doing push-ups. When I threw up my hands, it could have signaled, "Okay, I surrender" or "Back off," but within the context of the situation it was pretty obvious which one it was. It can be anything from a raised eyebrow to getting up and walking out of the room.

Probably the grandest gesture I ever made happened so long ago that the National Basketball Association (NBA) and the American Basketball Association (ABA) had yet to merge. Before the ABA came along, the only leverage a player had was to sit out a year, but once there were two different leagues—and two different drafts—it became very competitive. This particularly galled the NBA because the upstart ABA was consistently overpaying for the top draft choices in order to establish their league's credibility.

One year we received a very aggressive offer from the ABA's Denver Nuggets, well above what the NBA team had offered. Then just as suddenly they withdrew it. It made no sense until we received information that the two leagues were secretly talking merger and that Denver was one of the four ABA teams that were being considered. The NBA had obviously pressed Denver into dropping their lucrative offer for their number one draft choice, Marques Johnson, UCLA player of the year.

When I learned about this, I was furious, so I went to Williams & Connolly, the best antitrust law firm in Washington, D.C., and had them draw up a twenty-five-page antitrust lawsuit for eliminating competition. I then called the NBA commissioner at the time, Lawrence (Larry) O'Brien, and set up a meeting.

O'Brien was as tough as nails. He had previously worked in the Johnson administration, and for that, believe me, you had to be tough. I steeled my nerves, walked into O'Brien's office, pulled this document out of my briefcase, and handed it to him. "Here is our antitrust complaint against the league," I said. "We haven't filed it yet, and we don't want to file it. But if you don't force the league to do what's right, I promise you we are going to file it exactly one week from today."

Within a matter of days the NBA team that had drafted our player upped its offer to match Denver's original offer before it was withdrawn. I later learned that O'Brien had extracted a "merger tax" from all the other NBA teams in order to make up the difference between the two offers.

COVER ALL YOUR BASES
Michael Fuchs

Fuchs is an executive producer and former CEO for HBO.

My advice is to leave no stone unturned. One of my favorite deals happened when I was a CEO at HBO. The network decided to organize a heavyweight championship elimination tournament as a big television event. This would allow us to control, contract-wise, the heavyweight division. We got all the major candidates to sign on.

I had been aware of a boxer we had not tried to sign, a young kid by the name of Mike Tyson, who was about eighteen years old at the time and had fought once or twice on the old ABC Saturday afternoon boxing shows. I convinced everyone at HBO to let him in the tournament by asking, "What would happen if this kid really turned out to be something and we didn't have him in our tournament? It would undermine the whole credibility of our efforts."

We contacted Jimmy Jacobs and Bill Clayton, his managers at the time, and after several days of hellish negotiations, because Jimmy and Bill were notoriously tough, we got Tyson into the tournament. He won the tournament and became the youngest heavyweight champion in history—and spurred an enormous ratings bonanza at HBO for years after that. ∎

How I Got "Edged"

It is obvious that my company, ProServ, and IMG were always fierce competitors. For many years the head of IMG's tennis division was a fellow named H. Kent (Bud) Stanner, one of the best "talkers" I've ever met. He would lie straight to your face, but somehow you couldn't get mad at him. (Someone else at IMG once told me that the name of an important person once came up in a meeting, and Stanner referred to him as one of his "best friends." Someone else in the meeting said, "That's funny. He said he's never met you." Without skipping a beat, Stanner replied, "Phone friends. We're best phone friends.")

On one particularly embarrassing occasion I flew to Dallas to meet with the number one amateur player in America after an awards dinner. Before the dinner I ran into Stanner in the men's room. Out of nowhere he said, "I suppose you're here to see so-and-so?" I said I was, and Stanner said, "Oh, that's too bad. We signed him this afternoon." Like a complete idiot I turned around and flew back to Washington the next morning.

A few months later I ran into this player and asked him, "How could you sign with IMG back in Dallas without even giving us a chance to meet with you?" He looked at me curiously and said, "I'm not sure what you mean. I signed with IMG only last week." Stanner has never let me live that one down.

8

MAKE YOUR WORDS COUNT

I have a friend who has a little boy in nursery school. Whenever he or any of his other classmates start to go at each other, the teacher (after separating them) says, "Use your words! Use your words!" meaning, "Explain yourself in a reasonable manner rather than beating up on each other." I think that's pretty good advice for adults as well.

Consider, for instance, the 2008 Democratic Party primary, where Hillary Clinton, in attempting to explain away one of her several gaffes, said that with the millions of words coming out of her mouth, it was all but inevitable that she would occasionally misspeak and that she should therefore not be held accountable for everything she says.

Nonsense. Compare that to "I give you my word" or "A man's word is his bond." "Word" literally becomes a synonym for honesty and integrity.

Words matter. I like to negotiate a deal in person if possible and rarely agree to negotiate over the phone and never via email, because I need to see the other person, read his body language, watch his eyes, and listen to his inflection. But nothing is more important than the words that come out of my mouth. It's words on which your character is judged and by which others determine if you can be trusted—if you are "as good as your word."

I have also found time and again that the way you couch what you say or the tone or inflection you give it can make all the difference in the world. I have a friend who I don't think has ever used the phrase "I disagree" in his life. Instead he says something like "I would argue that . . ." or "I'd make the case for . . ." When someone says, "I disagree," I have seen the other party flinch slightly, but how my friend says it often isn't even perceived as a negative comment.

Have Some Fun

I believe the ability to find humor in a situation and the ability to be able to laugh at oneself are invaluable assets not just in business but in life. Humor is a tension breaker, and it has actually been proven that it will help you live longer!

One of my legendary liabilities is that I am often late for

appointments, so often that a friend of mine once had a T-shirt printed up for me that read THIS IS THE EARLIEST I'VE EVER BEEN LATE. It is certainly not intentional on my part, and I know it can really anger people, but as much as I have tried to change, I still have a hard time showing up on time. (I should have tried to do more business in southern Europe or South America, where almost everyone shows up late and no one cares.) Maybe this is why I need to have a sense of humor about myself. If I got uptight every time I was going to be late, I'd be dead by now.

I also don't think humor has ever cost me a deal or a relationship. Recently, I met a colleague in New York, and together we were going to take a taxi downtown for a very important meeting. I showed up late (with a valid excuse: My plane got hung up on the tarmac in D.C.), and my colleague didn't make much of an effort to hide his irritation. It got worse when we tried to hail a cab—in midtown Manhattan, in midday traffic, with heavy rain coming down. My colleague was literally standing in the middle of the street dodging cars and trying to find a cabdriver to bribe, when he turned around and looked at me with absolute disgust.

And I started to laugh. We both looked like drowned rats who were trying their best to get run over. "Come on," I shouted to him. "This isn't so bad. Let's have some fun."

When we got into a cab, my colleague said to me, "That's why I hate you and that's why I love you, Donald. Every time I'm ready to kill you, you make me laugh." I had come up with the right words at the right time. Of course, because of the horrible weather, the other people were also late, and as it turned out, the meeting could not have gone any better.

Don't Let Them See You Mad

Visibly losing your temper during the dealmaking process is almost always a very bad idea. Think about it: Whatever is making you so upset is inevitably something that is particularly important to you, and everyone in the room gets to see exactly what that is when you start losing it. When you lose your temper, you also lose leverage. All your cards are on the table, and the other side gains the advantage.

In 2007, I had been trying to recruit the United States' fastest rising tennis star, Donald Young, who is gangly and looks like a frisky newborn colt out on the court. This makes him very appealing to watch, and I believed he had superstar potential.

When I arrived in Atlanta to meet with Donald and his parents, I immediately sensed a negative feeling in the air, which was confirmed almost from the moment I introduced myself. First, Donald spent all of twenty minutes in the meeting before he said he had to go. And then his mother said, "You don't even remember meeting me the first time when you were down here just a few weeks ago."

Something snapped inside me. Suddenly I was furious, and I came back at Donald's mom with both guns blazing. "Of course I remember meeting you, Mrs. Young," I said, "but the first time wasn't three weeks ago. It was at the French Open two years ago when we were sitting together watching your son in the juniors get mad at his doubles partner and intentionally tank the third set. I didn't bring it up earlier because I didn't want to embarrass you with your son's behavior."

Needless to say, the meeting ended shortly thereafter. Also needless to say, we don't represent Donald Young. In fact, as it turned out, he ended up signing with Octagon, our business competitor. Not only did my show of anger ruin any chance I had with the Youngs, but it was a low point for me personally. Usually after getting angry I feel embarrassed at the very least and regret my actions.

When You Have Nothing to Lose

Although I would put this technique in the "Don't try this at home" category, there have been a couple of times where anger has actually worked in my favor. The one and only time I would ever recommend showing your anger is when you're confident you can put a cap on it and when you have absolutely nothing to lose.

Earlier I mentioned that when I had to pull Stan Smith out of a package endorsement deal with Converse, they refused to do business with me or ProServ or any of our players for several years. During this period I heard from a number of sources that the marketing director was trashing us at any opportunity he could get. One day the new president asked me why we never did business together. "Why would I ever deal with a company that is constantly going around bad-mouthing us?" I said politely but with an inescapable tone of anger. This was news to him, and that's what ended our "cold war" with Converse.

"Do You Have the Authority to Make This Deal?"

I have a lawyer friend who keeps a stuffed monkey on his bookshelf. Whenever he senses during a phone conversation that someone is about to hedge his bets by saying something like "I'll need to get back to you," he says, "Let me check that out with my monkey." It's his odd little way of letting the other party know that *he* knows the other party is trying to leave himself an out.

"Do you have the authority to make this deal?" is something I say all the time if I have the slightest doubt that the person I'm talking to doesn't. It serves three purposes. First, if he doesn't have the authority, then what am I doing here? I have my client's authority, but both sides need to be able to make the deal; otherwise, I'm dealing with the wrong person.

Second, if the person says he does have the authority, it cuts out one of the more frequently used bet hedgers: "I need to check with so-and-so." It's my version of the stuffed monkey.

Third, and this happens frequently, the other party will say he has the authority even if he doesn't in order to save face. He then becomes your best advocate, because he doesn't want to embarrass himself by having to come back and say he did not have the authority after all.

About four years ago I had to renew Stan Smith's contract with Adidas. I wanted to renegotiate the contract. When Stan retired in 1978, I reluctantly agreed to switch from a 3 percent royalty on all Stan Smith shoes to a flat fee but with a ten-year contract. With the benefit of hindsight, it was a mistake, but who could have foreseen that Adidas would be selling eight different Stan Smith models thirty years later? I wasn't going to make the same mistake again, but I knew this would be a tough sell to Adidas.

Martin Brewer, the head of licensing, would have none of it. "Are you out of your mind?" he kept saying. "Stan is fifty-seven years old, and he hasn't had a royalty since back in the dark ages."

"Well," I said, "he's your oldest employee. He's been with Adidas longer than anyone—since 1972! What about loyalty?"

Admittedly, that was a bit weak, but I had very little leverage, so I kept saying over and over again, "But he's your oldest employee, and Adidas should honor his loyalty."

For six months nothing happened. Stan began to get nervous, but I told him that I didn't want him to sign until they agreed to give us a royalty. "After all," I said, "you're their oldest employee."

Then one day Brewer got interested in some other things, so he put his right-hand man on it to continue the talks. The first question I asked him was, "Do you have the authority to make this deal?"

"Absolutely," he said. "I have the authority."

So I said, "Did you know that Stan is your oldest employee?"

"I do know that," he said, "and I think it's fair that he should get a royalty." And just like that, he gave us a royalty!

We ended up signing a ten-year deal, and last year it produced well over half a million dollars in royalties for Stan. Not bad for a sixty-one-year-old tennis player. "You know," Stan said, "that's probably the best deal you ever did for me."

Today Martin Brewer is head of worldwide marketing for Adidas. Recently I saw him at the Davis Cup matches. He came over, and we shook hands. Then he said, "You know, Donald, I should never have given up the authority to make that deal—or, after ten years, given Stan that royalty." I just smiled.

Keep Saying No

This only applies in those situations where you're not even sure you want to make the deal or are leaning against it: Keep saying no, and it will act as a kind of tiebreaker.

When Jimmy Connors was ranked number one in the world, he was approached by Kellogg's Corn Flakes, who wanted to use his name in a TV commercial. Although it would not have involved any of Jimmy's time, which was a big priority for him, there is a finite list of endorsements a player can make without ruining both his credibility and his marketability. Kellogg's also wanted to pay a flat fee, as opposed to residuals, and the fee was so marginal that we turned them down.

They immediately doubled their offer. We said no again, and they immediately doubled it again.

So now we did some investigating. As it turned out, the ad agency had done its homework and had come up with a list of superstar athletes who actually ate and liked Kellogg's Corn

Flakes, as opposed to just some endorsement deal—like putting the picture of the star-of-the-moment on the front of a box of Wheaties.

Now we realized we had a lot of leverage that we didn't know we had. First, there was a finite list of cornflakes-eating athletes, so it wasn't as if they could just say, "Okay, let's just get somebody else." Second, they had to be superstars with immediate name recognition. If they used mid-level athletes, the commercials obviously wouldn't work.

So we kept saying no. We ultimately ended up with five times the original offer.

Again, you have to be absolutely sure of your motives—that you're not saying no because you are simply angry or annoyed, and you're not saying no when you might really prefer to negotiate. Otherwise it's too risky as a strategy. Even one "no" could turn out to be one "no" too many, as in the game where you try to see who can toss a coin closest to the wall, but if your coin touches the wall, you lose. It's all or nothing. In other respects it's one of the best ways imaginable to find out how badly they really want the deal—as long as you have the edge.

9

RECOGNIZE YOUR LEVERAGE

Going into every deal, both sides have leverage. By definition, if you don't have something they want and they don't have something you want, there is absolutely no reason to get together in the first place. The art is in appreciating the leverage you have relative to theirs and understanding how to use it effectively.

The two previous chapters focused on what you might do or say to create an edge for yourself. But there are other times when your leverage develops during the course of negotiation or you discover leverage you didn't know you had, which is why I place such emphasis on being a good listener and having enough confidence and background knowledge to be able to think on your feet.

Sell to Their Emotions

Although most deals come down to money, it is important to be able to recognize when they don't. When someone's emotions are invested in whatever you're selling, use this as leverage. It is not about the money for someone who is sentimentally invested in your asset, but that doesn't mean it's not about the money for *you*. In these cases it is especially important to be honest and fair, but it's also important to recognize those rare times when what you have to offer means more to someone than any amount of money.

René Lacoste is one of France's fabled "Four Musketeers"—the tennis players whose statues stand at the French Open's Roland Garros tennis stadium, which was built so that spectators could watch the Davis Cup's Four Musketeers beat American players on a much slower red clay court. René is probably the most famous tennis player in French history. He was also the founder of one of the most venerable fashion brands, which bears his name.

When René was in his eighties, he always invited Jimmy Connors and me to his home for lunch during the French Open and would frequently mention Jimmy's weird-looking Wilson T2000 metal racket. I didn't understand why until years later, when I discovered that René owned the patent on that racket and was collecting a royalty on every one Wilson sold! No wonder he was so interested in the T2000.

Lacoste, to this day, is a family-owned and family-run business. When René died, Lacoste was taken over by his son Bernard, whom I got to know fairly well; he was one of the finest and most gracious gentlemen I have ever met. Several years ago Bernard contracted brain cancer and had to turn over the day-to-day running of the company to his brother, Michel.

One day I received a call from Bernard, who was barely working at this point, and he said to me, "You know, Donald, my father and I always wanted to sign Arthur Ashe, but we never even bothered to call you because he was always under contract with Adidas."

This absolutely shocked me. Neither Arthur nor I ever had a clue about this. Then Bernard added, "I think Andy Roddick can be the American we always wanted but never had."

Talk about leverage: "the American we always wanted but never had." I jumped on that one with both feet, and we ended up agreeing to a very lucrative long-term deal for Andy. Pretty soon I was on my way to France with Ken Meyerson, who handles Roddick's affairs, to finalize the contract. No sooner had we checked into the Intercontinental Hotel than I got a call from Bernard Lacoste, who wanted to get out of his sickbed and join us for lunch. When he arrived, he looked terrible, very pale and gaunt, but he said he wanted to call Andy in Texas to congratulate him, to tell him how pleased they all were, and to welcome him to the Lacoste family, which he did with great warmth in spite of his condition.

Sadly, Bernard died several months later, and Michel took over running the company. Before Bernard passed away, he had managed to fulfill a dream, not just for himself but also for his father. That dream was our leverage.

WHAT'S DRIVING THEM?

James Harmon

Harmon is the chairman and CEO of the financial advisory service Harmon & Co. He served as the chairman and president of the Export-Import Bank of the United States. He was also the chairman and CEO of Wertheim Schroder & Co. from 1986 to 1995, and the senior chairman until June 1997.

In trying to close any transaction, the most important factor is to ascertain the real goals of the other side. The key to accomplishing this is to listen. Often people will not want to say why they are doing a deal. Sometimes it's for liquidity purposes, sometimes it's for prestige, and sometimes it's out of necessity, but understanding what is driving the parties is crucial to negotiating a compromise. You may be surprised that money is usually not the only or even the paramount motivator in a deal.

It takes a very good listener to understand and analyze the other party. Listening is more important than talking—you don't learn anything when you're talking. After gathering all information possible, you also need to take the time to understand the background of the parties and business so that you can draw conclusions about why they want to do a transaction.

One of my best deals was when I was a partner at the bank Wertheim & Co. and negotiated a transaction with the British bank Schroders. The bank had plans to expand into the United States, and what I learned by listening was that the bank wasn't motivated by price. In fact, they did not want to bargain. Breaking into the U.S. market with an impeccable reputation was more important.

One day the chairman of Schroders said to me, "We should talk about what we would cut back on if there was ever an economic crisis."

I said, "I would cut out our dining rooms and cars for executives."

He responded, "Oh, Jim, that would be the last thing we would cut back. If you cut out the dining rooms and cars, everyone will know you are in trouble. I would rather cut out parts of the business."

That told me enough about how much image meant to my British partners. From there it was a guiding factor in much of the negotiations we had. I made sure that all of my Wertheim partners conducted themselves in a way that made the British feel they were associating with the highest-quality bankers. Making the most money was not as important to them as the image. As a result, we constructed a partnership instead of a straight sale. Even though my bank, Wertheim, was in fact liquidated, to the outside world it looked like a partnership. When the deal closed and Schroders came to the United States, they had the Wertheim name to back them. The bank has been Schroder Wertheim ever since. ■

Don't Discount the Little Guy

Whenever you think there is just one way out of a situation, think again. More often than not there will be a lesser-known option that you can use as leverage. If there's a company that is so successful it seems to have a monopoly in an area, there are probably dozens of other companies trying to take a piece of that lucrative business.

I was lucky that I learned this lesson without even having to lift a finger. Prior to the arrival at ESPN of John Skipper, with whom we made the U.S. Open deal, I had had a very contentious relationship with the network. In fact, almost everyone did. As far as cable sports television was concerned, they were the big man on campus, and they were often very arrogant about it.

I was renegotiating ESPN's rights to the French Open, an $18 million deal. It had gotten to the point where we were only $250,000 apart (pocket change considering the deal size), but ESPN managed to drag out these negotiations for nine months. Their whole attitude was "We're the only game in town. Dell has no place else to go, so eventually he's going to have to make this deal on our terms."

Then out of the blue I received a call from Ken Solomon, CEO of a new cable channel, Tennis Channel. Tennis Channel had a lot of money behind it and wanted to know what it would take to get the French Open away from ESPN.

I had been keeping the French Tennis Federation fully informed, so at this point they weren't too happy with ESPN either. At my suggestion Solomon immediately flew to Switzerland to meet with Michel Grach, the television director of the French Tennis Federation, while he was on vacation there with his family. The next day he concluded a deal with Tennis Channel for more than twice what ESPN had been offering.

Since Tennis Channel was new, we had certain built-in protections, such as a threshold for the number of subscribers before the next French Open and the number of broadcast hours, but here's the real kicker: The Federation agreed, for the first time ever, to give Tennis Channel the right to *sublicense* some of its rights to another cable network. Since ESPN had already been advertising itself as "The Grand Slam Network," it couldn't very well proceed without the French Open, so Tennis Channel ended up sublicensing ESPN half the TV rights for more money than it had been willing to pay us for *all* the rights!

"Reluctantly" Give Them What You Don't Need

In any negotiation both sides obviously need to walk away with something, and the sooner you can establish what the other side needs, the stronger your negotiating position is going to be. But I have often found that what may be extremely important to them may be relatively unimportant to us. By "giving in" on whatever points those happen to be, at the very worst you are going to gain some goodwill and most likely you are going to get something you really wanted, too, because of the perceived mutual sacrifice.

When Head, Arthur Ashe's first racket company, was sold to the larger sporting goods manufacturer, Head Sports Inc., owned by the conglomerate AMF, I remember that AMF wanted a "morals clause" in Arthur's contract, which is not all that uncommon, and we were happy to accommodate them. What was unusual was the language they used, which I found not only offensive but also downright racist.

They wanted Arthur to agree that he would never join the Black Panthers, which was very big at the time, that he would never foment racial unrest or start a race riot (!), and so on in that vein.

Arthur had always been a powerful presence in the battle for racial equality, but never in a strident or offensive way. I was almost ashamed to show him this clause, but when he saw it, he laughed.

"Starting a race riot is the last thing that would ever occur to me," he said, "so why would I care if it's in the contract or not?" Needless to say, we got other concessions for "reluctantly" going along with this language.

More recently when I was negotiating Andy Roddick's apparel deal with Lacoste, they threw me a real curve. We had started off discussing a three-year contract and had gotten the length up to five years with an option for the sixth year in Lacoste's favor, but then they said, "Suppose Andy starts to not play very well and slips out of the top rankings. He is not worth as much to us. We need to protect ourselves, so we want a clause in the contract that says if Andy drops out of the top fifteen in the rankings, we have the right to reduce the [mid-seven-figure] annual guarantee by 75 percent."

I have always maintained that brand-name athletes are just that—brands—and that their won/lost records, rankings, batting averages, completion percentages, and statistical measurements should have nothing to do with the contract, but privately I felt Lacoste had a point. Once a tennis player drops out of the top ten, his or her matches are less likely to be covered on television; in addition, there are fewer personal appearances and the press coverage is less.

Still, I felt it was something I needed to discuss with Andy, and when I did, I was shocked by his response. He just sort of laughed and said, "Hell, if I ever drop below number fifteen, I'm going to retire from tennis anyway, and Lacoste can do whatever it wants."

My first instinct had been to reduce the size of the drop in percentage and push the "fall below" ranking number up to twenty or twenty-five, but after speaking with Andy, I changed direction.

We ultimately "reluctantly" agreed to give Lacoste the reduction they were asking for, but in return we received (1) a larger annual guarantee and (2) an automatic contract extension in that sixth year if Andy was ranked in the top five.

In other words, we gave up something we didn't need in return for a couple of things that were great to have.

Let Them Do the Talking

Much of the time, you have to work to identify or create specific leverage before you go into a negotiation. But sometimes, especially in situations where you're dealing with many different departments that don't communicate with one another, if you let them talk, they will hand it to you on a silver platter. This is particularly true when you're dealing with big egos, which we often are. Give them enough rope, and they'll eventually tie a nice little noose for themselves.

Certainly the most advantageous negotiating position I've ever found myself in (or maybe anyone has ever found himself in) was Patrick Ewing's first contract with the New York Knicks. Not only did they hand us all our leverage on a silver platter, but they kept handing us silver platters.

First, the Knicks, who desperately needed a winning team, won the rights to Ewing in the first nationally televised draft lottery, so the whole country knew the Knicks absolutely had to make this deal. (The televised image of the Knicks' GM, Dave DeBusschere, winning the number one draft choice, clenching both fists, and coming out of his chair plays over and over again on New York sports television.) Next, the Knicks immediately began touting Patrick as "the savior," which, of course, the New York sports media ate up and promoted daily.

We had not even discussed Patrick's contract yet, when we were the beneficiaries of the most extraordinary request: The Knicks PR guy called me and asked if he could put Patrick's picture on the front of their season ticket brochure. I immediately said yes because I realized they had just handed me leverage. Now, if they didn't sign Patrick, they would have to destroy all their brochures and advertisements; otherwise it would be consumer fraud. Then, as if we needed any more leverage, Patrick had just signed a seven-figure deal with Adidas, which meant that if we had to, we could wait out the Knicks indefinitely.

Then came the icing on the cake. The Knicks were owned at the time by Gulf & Western, which was well known for being an incredibly arrogant company. One day I received a call from Gulf & Western's senior vice president asking me if we could come over that afternoon. When we got there, it became obvious that he had cut his basketball executives (including Dave DeBusschere) completely out of the negotiating process. We had been negotiating with them for three months, and now all of a sudden I got the feeling Gulf & Western wanted to finalize the contract in the next few hours.

He then said probably the dumbest thing I've ever heard in a negotiation: "I need to fly to Paris by five p.m. this afternoon, and I want to make this deal before I leave." Now we not only had all the leverage we could possibly have, but we also had time on our side. In other words, we didn't have to end up with an outrageous number; we could start out with one.

The end result? The year before, Hakeem Olajuwon had become the highest-paid player in the NBA at $1.2 million a year. Patrick's contract was for a ten-year guarantee in excess of $30 million, by far the richest deal in the history of the NBA at that time.

Don't Get Hung Up on What the Other Side Is Getting

There is no law that requires the other party to lay all their cards on the table, and often a key fact won't come out until the negotiation is over. How do you protect against this? You go in with a very clear idea of where you want to come out. What do you need to get out of the deal? If you get what you need or better, then it really doesn't matter how well the other side makes out.

When Jimmy Connors' racket deal came up for renewal, I found myself in the very odd position of negotiation with the former secretary of the treasury, William Simon, who had bought Wilson Sporting Goods in a private equity deal.

We had practically reached a deal with Wilson when we hit a speed bump over the assignment clause. The assignment clause, which is standard in most licensing agreements, allows the company to assign the contract to another party. I was not trying to take out the assignment clause, but a racket deal is obviously fairly important to the player, so I was negotiating some conditions that would allow Jimmy to have some input over the disposition of his contract.

That is when I received a call from Bill Simon, who said somewhat imperiously, "Look, we can't modify the assignment clause, but I'm not concerned with what this is going to cost us. We just need to get this deal done. Name your price."

What that said to me was that Simon was about to sell the company and needed to get the deal on the books, which gave us tremendous leverage.

I went back to Jimmy, and together we decided we would triple our asking price. They might be selling the company for hundreds of millions of dollars, but if we could get three times what we had originally asked for, then we were going to be pleased regardless.

"Done," said Simon. "Make the changes, have Connors sign the contract, and get it back to me right away."

About a month later it was announced that Wilson had been sold to a much larger Finnish company. Simon had needed the Connors contract as an asset and needed the right to assign it in order to make the deal happen.

If I had known for certain that the sale was about to take place, would it have changed anything? No. I think you really need to look at what you want to get out of the deal rather than what the other side is going to make or have to give up.

Ironically, if Simon had been more forthcoming about the sale, I'm not sure we would have had as much leverage. The conversation probably would have focused more on satisfying the assignment clause rather than what Wilson was willing to pay.

Get Lucky

Leverage can be a fickle thing. Just when you think you have all the leverage, bang, circumstances change. But sometimes this can work for you as well. When you get lucky, just thank the deal gods and move on. Luck has a way of evening up, so take it when you can get it.

In our business our clients are like our extended family. From the Saturday morning Coach Dean Smith called me at my home and asked if I would like to represent Michael Jordan in his NBA career, we treated Michael with extraordinary care. However, much has been written about Michael's gambling habits. One day he came to me and said he owed someone a lot of money. He asked me to make out a ProServ check for the guy to whom he owed the money, and he would then reimburse us. I was not going to say no, but I did ask him why this check could not be taken directly from his own account. "Because it is money I lost playing golf," he said, "and I want to keep it under the radar."

I wrote out the check, but six months later the person I had made it out to was indicted for income tax evasion in North Carolina. Needless to say, I was quite concerned. Once the trial started, it was going to look bad for Michael to testify and it was going to look even worse for me if I had to explain that Pro-Serv check. Obviously this was a very uncomfortable and ticklish situation for both of us. But two weeks into the trial, before either of us had to testify, the indicted individual died of a heart attack! His unfortunate death saved us both from future embarrassment.

Be Their Partner

Sometimes the other side has all the leverage, just by virtue of whom you happen to be dealing with. If you can become their partner, then their leverage becomes your leverage.

One of the peculiar things about the global sports business

is that there are certain people who virtually own sports in their part of the world. The late Kerry Packer, for instance, owned the largest television network in Australia and monopolized sports television there as a result. Fortunately, he was a great guy, but even if he had been a jerk, you didn't want to be his adversary. You wanted to be his partner because of the assets and leverage he brought to the table.

With people this powerful in your particular industry, all their leverage comes simply from who they are. Essentially what you want to do is let them conduct both sides of any negotiation— all very collegially—because otherwise they can roll over you if they choose to.

Like Kerry Packer, Jorge Paulo Lemann is a really good person. He is also arguably the most powerful businessman in Brazil. One of his companies, InBev, is the one that acquired Budweiser in 2008. We had been originally introduced through mutual friends. Jorge had been a player on Switzerland's Davis Cup team many years ago and had played at Harvard when I played at Yale, so once I tapped into those commonalities, we had an immediate rapport.

Recently I dropped Jorge a note saying that I was going to be in São Paulo the following week and would love to get together for lunch. He immediately wrote back saying that I must stay with him at his home while I was there.

When I got to São Paulo, the first thing he said to me was, "Donald, we must play some tennis." I was so out of shape that I tried to beg off, but he was insistent. He destroyed me on his backyard clay court, 6–2, 6–1. When we went up to the net to shake hands, he said to me, "Now we're even." He could see I had no idea what he was talking about, so he added with a laugh, "You beat me in the first round at Wimbledon thirty years ago, and I've been waiting to get my revenge ever since!"

Over the course of the next couple of days Jorge said to me, "Donald, we really need to do something together here in Brazil—some tennis events, some marketing, some television." Since we had never done business with each other before, I didn't know if he was serious or just trying to be nice. But recently, while I was in Miami, I ran into Nelson Aerts, one of Jorge's tennis partners. "Donald," he said, "Jorge really wants us to make this happen."

When I got back to the office, the first thing I did was call Ken Meyerson, the former head of our tennis division. "Ken," I said, "I don't care what you have to do or how you have to do it, but let's make this friendly deal in Brazil."

What comes out of it remains to be seen, but in Brazil I'd rather be seen with Jorge than anyone else. As a result, we formed a partnership with Nelson Aerts's company, Try Sports, to recruit young Brazilian players, organize events, and establish a national tennis center for all juniors to come and play as well as attend school. It is now called the National Tennis Center of Brazil and all of it is backed by Jorge.

Just Go with the Flow

As the earlier story in this chapter about Ken Solomon flying to Switzerland to meet with the French Tennis Federation demonstrates, one of the most effective dealmaking techniques is just to get up and go. And the quicker you leave ("I'm on my way to the airport right now") and the farther you need to travel to get there, the more effective it often is.

On the other side of the coin, anytime you are operating outside your usual habitat—your geographic comfort zone—you probably lose a little leverage, often just from the logistics alone. (There are even television commercials about this in which a guy arrives all disoriented and disheveled for a meeting because he had a bad flight.)

I've made deals all over the world in some very exotic locales, but none more exotic—or disorienting—than the day I flew to meet with the sheik of Dubai.

The sheik had decided—this was quite a few years ago—that he wanted to create a tennis tournament and had contacted us to help him out. On the flight over I stopped briefly in Saudi Arabia and learned that King Faisal had just been assassinated, apparently by a distraught nephew who walked in and shot him dead with a pistol. That did nothing to help my comfort zone.

When we landed in Dubai, we were taken directly to a very large tent 20 miles out in the desert. Inside the tent the sheik was meeting with his subjects, who came before him to ask him for favors or to settle disputes. Everyone was on high alert, and sitting around the tent were also a lot of men holding rifles and

TIMING IS EVERYTHING

Stan Smith

Smith is a former professional tennis player who was ranked number one in the world in 1972.

When making a deal, I think that you have to know the market and the leverage that is available. Timing is the key to this; sometimes it is something that can be controlled, and sometimes it isn't. I know that when I won Wimbledon, I had great leverage and the time was ideal for talking to Adidas about putting my name on the first leather tennis shoe. Adidas wanted to get a foothold in the U.S. market, and by winning Wimbledon I solidified my position as the number one player in the United States.

The Adidas deal is by far the best that I have ever had. The shoe became very popular for tennis players around the world. It also happened to have a very plain white classic look, which helped generate tremendous long-term success.

The shoe is now being made in many different colors, materials, and designs and marketed as a fashion shoe as well as a performance tennis shoe. The performance shoes have come a long way in design since 1971. They offer much more support and are much more appropriate for movements on the tennis court. This is one of those long-term deals that turned out really well because of the product, my nationality, and the timing of the original agreement. ∎

wearing bandoliers across their chests. It was like a scene out of an Arabian rewrite of *The Godfather*.

I felt pretty edgy myself. Soon we were led into a separate chamber behind the sheik's throne. We had been waiting there for about five minutes when all of a sudden I heard a very loud *pop!* As soon as I heard it, I hit the floor as though my life depended on it, which I thought it did.

I had just worked my way behind a couch when the sheik walked in. "I'm sorry for the shock," he said, looking a little bemused at seeing me on the floor, "but that was a lightbulb in here that just exploded."

That's leverage. I had long given up on any pretense of detachment and would have agreed to anything the sheik had to say. Fortunately, he was a very polite, decent man and didn't try to take advantage of the situation. He probably already knew that if the going got tough, I'd dive for the couch.

10

NEVER MAKE THE
FIRST OFFER

There is so much that goes into every deal—from a company's leverage, to reputation, to a single dealmaker's having a bad day. But as you home in on a specific deal you want to make and prepare for the negotiating room, everything becomes a bit more precise and more cemented. This chapter offers my nine chronological steps to seeing a deal from start to finish.

Step 1: Establish Relationships and Build Trust

This step, addressed in earlier chapters, is so incredibly important to finalizing a deal that I included it on the list even though it has already been covered. If you haven't earned the trust of the other people in the room, then coming to an agreement is going to be next to impossible.

Dean Smith, the now-retired basketball coach at the University of North Carolina at Chapel Hill, is not only the second-winningest coach (behind Bobby Knight) in the history of college basketball but also, along with John Wooden, among the most respected and beloved. He is also someone to whom I owe much of my success.

Coach Smith always had his players' backs and their best interests at heart. I met him through my older brother, who had played varsity tennis at UNC and had arranged for me to meet him and discuss representing some of his players. He never gave us a preferred position, but he did give us an opportunity to prove ourselves to him: He told us that if we stayed away from the campus and no one from our company called or bothered any of his players, when the season ended he would give us the same reward he offered to everyone else who followed these rules—meeting his players in his office.

By keeping our word, following his rules, and getting good deals for some of his players, we began to earn Coach Smith's trust. One of our earlier UNC clients, Phil Ford, went number two in the NBA draft. During the Dean Smith years we signed twenty to twenty-five of his best players, including Michael Jordan, who surprisingly went number three in the draft, not number one. A year later we made our usual one-day visit to the UNC campus, but this time it was followed by an unusual phone call from Coach Smith a few weeks later. That year James Worthy was coming out of UNC to turn pro, and he was projected to go number one in the NBA draft. "I want you to call James," Coach Smith said, "and go back down to sign him."

I couldn't believe what I was hearing, so I asked him why. "Because," Coach Smith said, "I think he's about to sign with someone I don't trust. James's father is very religious, and this guy, Tom Collins, uses religion effectively in recruiting. I'm afraid James may end up signing with him for all the wrong reasons."

So I called James and agreed to meet him in a motel room near the Chapel Hill campus. It seemed very strange. I had no idea what Coach Smith had told James about why we were having this meeting. The other problem was that his father came along with him! I really didn't know what to say or do. There was an NBA playoff game on the television, so the three of us were just sitting there making small talk and watching the game, when Mr. Worthy excused himself to go to the bathroom. As soon as the bathroom door closed, James said to me, "Do you have the contract with you?"

"Yes, I do," I said. "It's right here in my coat pocket."

"Give it to me and let me sign it right now while my father is still in the bathroom."

"What are we going to tell your father?" I asked.

"Don't worry about it," James said. "Don't tell him anything. Coach said he'll take care of it."

And that was the last I heard of it. James Worthy did indeed go number one in the draft that year, and we represented him. Because we had established a relationship and trust with Coach Smith, the "negotiation" was seamless.

Step 2: Evaluate Your Opponent

Now that you're finally at the negotiating table, forget for just a moment all the clutter and detail relating to the deal. Just for a moment size up the other side to see if they're alert and sharp and ready to make something happen. If something seems off about the person on the other side of that table, there's a good chance the deal is not going to go through no matter how hard you try.

One example of things seeming not quite right during bargaining was Andy Roddick's non-deal with Reebok. Andy had had a relationship with Reebok—shoes and apparel—since he was a teenager. It wasn't a great deal, so we wanted considerably more money, some flexibility, and a longer contract, particularly after Andy won the U.S. Open in 2003.

We were having trouble getting any traction, so I called Paul Fireman, founder and chairman of Reebok, directly. It was right before Christmas and everything was pretty much shut down, but I managed to reach him at his vacation home in Palm Beach.

Paul said, "Donald, I really want to get this done. I'm going to send my plane and fly you down here right away." So that same day I hopped on Paul's plane—it was just me and the flight attendant. In a matter of hours we got most of the deal done, and it was a really good one for Andy—a low seven-figure advance but with a lot of escalators, and it stretched out for ten years. The most attractive aspect was that if Andy performed at a certain level, a royalty deal on shoes and clothing would kick in.

I'd say we were 90 percent there when Paul said, "I want you to finish this up with Tom Shine [who usually handled all the major contract negotiations for Reebok]. As you know, he has my authority to make the deal."

When I got back, I sat down with Andy and thoroughly went over each point in the agreement with him. Then I called his parents and did the same thing. In the meantime, I couldn't get Tom Shine on the phone. In my experience deals have a certain arc, and I could feel this one starting to fade away because of Tom's silence.

I decided I'd better fly up to Reebok in Boston. I called Paul Fireman, and he said, "If you want to come up, I'd be happy to see you, but if you're coming up to talk about Andy Roddick, don't come. You are supposed to be dealing with Tom Shine."

I flew up anyway and learned I had been right to suspect something was up. Paul said, "Look, I'm sorry, but we just can't do this deal—it's too expensive!"

Fortunately, in a panic I had already contacted Nike and, later, Lacoste, and Reebok's backing out eventually led to a much better deal with Lacoste. But I still didn't know why the men at Reebok were acting so strange. It wasn't like Paul to back out of a deal.

Six weeks later it was announced that Reebok was being acquired by Adidas! I called Paul and asked him, "Did this acquisition have anything to do with your getting cold feet with Andy?"

"Of course," he said. "I was trying to sell the company. I couldn't show an expensive deal or liability on my balance sheet that stretched out for ten years."

What could I have done about it? Nothing—except read my opponents and get my backup plan together. You may go into a deal with a ton of enthusiasm, but if you can't see any desire from the other side, you probably aren't going to get what you want.

Step 3: Use Targeted Knowledge

You can do all the preparatory research in the world, but unless you're able to utilize the information as the negotiation is going on, it's useless to you. It is really important to identify what type of information will be useful to you when you're ready to make the deal, and to have that specific information on hand (and memorized) during negotiations.

One way of knowing what is important is to think about the future. Unless otherwise stated, deals stretch out indefinitely, so you have to think about what you can make from this deal years down the line.

Another way of knowing what is important is to think what the deal is going to look like down the line. Will it look just as good ten years later as it did the day of the agreement?

Step 4: Never Make the First Offer (Except When You Should)

Why do you want them to make the first offer? Because you are really not seeking an offer at all; you are seeking information. The first offer gives you an insight into their thought process. It crystallizes all their thinking up to that point and boils it down to a single number or a series of deal points. It also tells you what their primary issues are. Whatever terms they throw in along with their first number are often the most important issues to them.

Generally, most people won't fight you when it comes to making the first offer. But when they do resist, you must hold your ground.

Back in the early 1980s we represented a young basketball player by the name of Kermit Washington, who was drafted in the first round by the Los Angeles Lakers. Kermit would later become infamous for breaking another player's jaw (Rudy

Tomjanovich) and ending his career. They occasionally still show the punch on television, which is a shame, because Kermit is also a really good person and was a great basketball player—a great rebounder and passer.

The owner of the Los Angeles Lakers at the time was Jack Kent Cooke, but we were in the office of the Lakers' GM, Fred Schaus, when we asked him for his opening offer. He said, "Donald, you know that Jack won't ever allow us to make the first offer" (which is another negotiating tactic: "The guy who's not here in the room won't let me do this").

I was silent for a moment and then said, "Fred, I happen to know that isn't true. We've got all day and all tomorrow if you'd like. We can talk about the weather or movies or your sex life, whatever you want, but we're not going any further until you make an opening offer."

It became comical. We sat there in silence for what seemed like an eternity, although it was probably only a couple of minutes before we both chuckled. Finally Fred said, "Okay, Donald. You win. Here's our opening offer . . ."

Then there's the exception: If you suspect you're going to get lowballed and the offer will be much lower than what you hope to get, make the first offer. The idea here is that you'll raise the bar and close the distance between the two of you. You'll never have to entertain the insulting first offer, because you anticipated it coming and simply skipped right over it. Knowledge of an impending lowball offer is so helpful, in fact, that I'm not above doing almost anything to find out what their first offer is going to be before they've actually made it.

When we were doing the second Michael Jordan contract with the Chicago Bulls, I was sitting across the desk from Jerry Reinsdorf, the Bulls' notoriously tough managing partner, when Jerry excused himself to take a phone call in the corner. While he was on the phone, I leaned across his desk to sneak a peek at the paper in front of him. The number at the top of the page was $4 million, which wasn't even close to what we were thinking (a $40-to-$50-million range). I had made some rough notes on a yellow legal pad, so as soon as Jerry got off the phone, I tore off the top page and handed it to him. "Here, let me show you our 'offer sheet.' We're at the $52 million range."

When I made that $52 million offer, it obviously wasn't the number I was ultimately shooting for. After all, it was a negotiation, and both sides are going to have to give. When it comes down to money, don't counter with what you hope to get; counter with a higher number that you hope will get you where you want to end up. In other words, if they offer ten and you want twenty, counter with thirty. This too-high offer establishes the upper end of a bracket that is going to be reduced. This may seem self-evident, but I can't tell you how many times I have seen people, including myself occasionally, name the number I want and then be shocked when it is not immediately accepted. It is much easier to compromise than it is to defend your initial numbers hoping the other party will see the wisdom of your ways.

HAVE SPECIFIC OBJECTIVES
George Mitchell

Mitchell is a former United States senator who currently serves as chairman of the worldwide law firm DLA Piper and also as the chancellor of Queen's University Belfast, in Northern Ireland. He was the U.S. Senate majority leader from 1989 to 1995 and chairman of The Walt Disney Company from March 2004 until January 2007. President Obama recently chose him to be the American special envoy to the Middle East.

The most important aspect of making a deal is understanding clearly in advance what your bottom line is and being prepared to close the deal once you've achieved it. In other words, be able to quit while you're ahead. I've seen many negotiations founder because one or more parties didn't have at the outset a clear picture of what would satisfy them. Too often the approach is to "get as much as you can" or to "win it all." These vague objectives are rarely satisfied and often hard to quantify under the pressure of time-limited discussions.

I don't think of it as a "deal," but the most gratifying negotiation I've been involved in was in Northern Ireland. There, over a five-year period, I chaired three sets of discussions and negotiations, which led to the Good Friday peace agreement of 1998. It was a difficult, complex, and emotional situation. A bitter sectarian conflict had raged for many years, killing thousands and injuring tens of thousands. In the main negotiation there were twelve participants: the governments of Ireland and the United Kingdom and ten political parties from Northern Ireland. It took months to agree on a set of rules, more months to agree on an agenda, and then more than a year to get an agreement. All the while there were many acts of violence—bombings and assassinations—by those who opposed the peace process and sought to disrupt it. But in the end, thanks to the courage of the political leaders of Northern Ireland, the United Kingdom, and Ireland, an agreement was reached and the war ended. Now, in the Northern Ireland Assembly, the elected representatives of the people debate the ordinary issues of life in a democratic society: education, health care, agriculture, economic growth, etc., and life is returning to normal. There are still problems, of course. But they're the problems every society faces. And they're being settled by ballots, not bullets. That's truly gratifying. ■

Step 5: Be Creative

Now you have it: An offer is on the table. This is the time to remember why you got involved in the negotiation in the first place. This is also one of those points in the negotiation where you can get creative. Think of all the possible ways of getting what you want. If your opponent is willing to offer some kind of fair deal but can't, for example, pay you as much as you hoped, ask yourself if your opponent has any other assets that you'd be willing to trade for. If both parties see a benefit and trust one another, a creative or unusual deal is a serious possibility.

Many years ago—this goes back almost twenty-five years—we approached *Newsweek* magazine about being the title sponsor of a small tennis tournament in Palm Springs, California. One of the most common excuses I hear for not doing something is "We don't have the budget for that," but in the *Newsweek* case I felt it happened to be true.

So I got creative. What did *Newsweek* have that I wanted? An unlimited supply of ad pages. It is common practice now, not only in the tennis industry but in others. What we ended up doing was swapping the title sponsorship for $500,000 in advertising pages that we could sell to other companies. We were the first to use this ad sales approach.

With the *Newsweek* offer in hand, the smaller sponsorships became a lot easier to sell because we could throw a full-page ad into the mix. The *Newsweek* Open ran successfully for several years, and we sold out our ad pages every year.

Step 6: Listen for What They Need

In the previous chapter I talked about the importance of having a very clear picture of what, worst case, you need to get out of the deal. By the same token you also need to figure out what the other side needs in order to walk away as well. If both sides aren't satisfied, the deal is not going to happen even if there is an offer sitting on the table.

When I was called in to mediate the naming rights deal between the Washington Redskins and Federal Express, it was because, after five meetings, and even after a draft contract, negotiations had fallen through and recriminations had followed between the parties. This was no surprise. FedEx is like Nike or Disney—tough as nails, because as far as they're concerned they're the only game in town; and the Redskins' owner, Dan Snyder, is, well, Dan Snyder—smart, cagey, and impatient.

I was called in not only because I was friends with Fred Smith at FedEx, but because I was part of the team that did the first naming rights deal in the country, the Staples Center in Los Angeles.

The Staples Center naming rights came about after a discussion that one of our associates had in the office of the chairman of Staples, Tom Stemberg. The conversation started over what at the time was called the Los Angeles Coliseum. Tom had noticed that four different highways intersected right in front of the building, and it hit him that if companies paid a lot of money to put their names on buildings, why wouldn't they pay a lot of money to put their names on a sports arena? Stemberg, who was looking for more of a presence on the West Coast, jumped right away. Then it occurred to him: What was Staples getting for its money? In response we came up with a list of nineteen items that spelled out exactly what he was getting, and that list served as a template for several other naming deals, such as the Philips Arena in Atlanta and FedExField in Washington, D.C.

When I took over the Redskins negotiation, Snyder told me he wanted me to deal with only his partner, Fred Drasner, who was a Washington lawyer and was also the publisher of the New York *Daily News*.

While on a flight to New York to meet with Fred, I pulled out a yellow legal pad and recalled sixteen of the nineteen points that were part of the Staples Center deal. I then gave this to Fred in his apartment. He took one look at the list, crossed through two of them, and handed it back to me.

I said, "Can I take these fourteen items back to FedEx?"

He said, "Of course. That's our deal." And that was our deal. We had laid out item by item exactly what FedEx was getting for its money. In fact, because only a few have ever seen a naming deal list of benefits, I am going to reproduce that list here.

1. Four signs, permanent fixture, on each side of building
2. 40 ft by 120 ft banner on tower, wording at FedEx's discretion
3. 3000 ft × 10 ft windscreen around stadium
4. Signage in all parking areas
5. Name/logo on concession items
6. Sideline signage
7. FedEx logo on all event staffing
8. Naming rights at all press conferences
9. Access road to be named "FedEx Boulevard"
10. Directional signage out of stadium
11. Name to be called "FedExField" everywhere
12. FedEx named "official carrier of the Washington Redskins"
13. Year-round suite usage and club seating for all events
14. Penalty clause if stadium and field are not maintained in first-class fashion

A second list of additional benefits was added later, including billboards on Redskins television shows, two commercials, backdrop banner at press conferences, promotions via jumbotrons, some FedEx signage when rotational signage is in resting state, Internet presence, and so on.

What these lists did was allow us to discuss and lay out exactly what FedEx was getting out of this $205 million deal so they could feel confident about the money they were spending.

Just as the above list implies, deals don't have to be complicated. Most can be reduced to a single list on a single page. I am a great believer in deal memos and short-form agreements. In fact, my favorite line in a contract is "All parties will agree to use their best efforts to sign a long-form agreement by [insert date]." But they rarely do. In fact, NBC's initial $20 million agreement to broadcast the French Open started out and ended up as four pages.

Step 7: Keep It Simple

When all the details make a situation overwhelming, think of the main points of the deal, your main goals, and the big picture. Most deals are very simple. Whether you are doing a licensing agreement, selling a house, buying a car, or even making a deal to write a book, there are maybe six to eight crucial points to negotiate, and everything else is pretty much boilerplate. And just because a deal is twice as big, it doesn't have to be twice as complicated. Don't find things to squabble over simply because you think that's the responsible thing to do.

Keeping it simple is one of the ways to maintain your equilibrium during a deal. Obviously, the simpler your deal is, the less chance there is of your getting confused or off track.

One of the most famous tennis matches of all time was between Arthur Ashe, who was near the end of his career, and Jimmy Connors, who was in his prime, in the 1975 Wimbledon finals. The match was supposed to be a laugher for Connors. In fact, Ladbrokes, the British bookmaker, had made Arthur a sixteen-to-one underdog.

At dinner the night before the finals, Arthur and I talked very little about tennis except for one moment when we went over a few simple things about playing Connors: serve him wide in the deuce court; chip low to his forehand; keep the ball soft and slow with no pace; bring him to the net; and stay focused. The next morning I wrote down the five things we had gone over the night before and slipped the piece of paper into Arthur's mailbox at the Westbury Hotel.

Once the match began, Arthur somehow managed to win the first set easily. But the announcers were all talking about Arthur's demeanor during the changeovers. He was sitting completely still, and his head was bent down as though he were praying.

One of the announcers said, "He seems to be meditating. I think he's put himself in some kind of trance!"

Arthur went on to win the match in four sets, which was one of the greatest upsets in Wimbledon history, and Arthur's demeanor during changeovers never altered. It became a big story. That evening I asked him, "What the hell were you doing on the changeovers?" At first he looked at me kind of puzzled, but then he said, "Oh, that. Just before I went on the court, I put your note in my tennis bag, and on the changeovers I kept staring at the five things you had written down." So Arthur wasn't meditating at all—although I suppose that reading the same five things over and over again could put you into a kind of Zen-like state.

The point of this story is that whether it is tennis or deal-making or pretty much anything else in life, keep it simple.

When a deal requires you to get creative, start with the basics. Until you have that "simple" idea—that one driving force behind your deal—you won't be effective, and most likely you'll end up forgetting what you wanted out of the deal anyway.

That is exactly what happened with Michael Jordan's Air Jordan deal. Amid all sorts of complications, it was a simple slogan that saved the day. Michael had worn Converse all through his college years at the University of North Carolina, and everyone assumed that he was probably going to sign with Converse. We were holding out for a royalty and a line of sports apparel. Converse was offering neither, so we set up a meeting with Nike. In those days Nike was somewhat smaller in basketball shoes and was an afterthought for us. It occurred to me that if they might not want to spend enough money to compete with Converse, perhaps they would be more open to a royalty deal on shoes.

They weren't. There were four of us in my office on a Saturday morning, and we really weren't getting anywhere. We wanted a royalty on a line of Jordan shoes. They wanted the Nike line endorsed by Jordan. Everyone was talking at one another rather than to one another. Nike had been my backup plan, and now my backup plan was at an impasse.

Suddenly, from out of the blue, Peter Moore, who worked for Nike, blurted out, "What about 'Air Jordan'?" Everyone stopped and just looked at one another. Finally someone said, "That's perfect!" After that, the royalty deal could not get done fast enough. Of course, Air Jordan went on to become the biggest licensing deal in sports history, and all it took was two words, a simple concept that embodied everything Jordan and Nike needed.

Step 8: Listen for the Moment of Truth and Be Prepared to Walk Away

If you are almost certain that those on the other side have gone as far as they can go and you know what you need out of the deal but there is still a gap, this is your moment of truth. And if it's just not attainable, you have to be prepared to walk away.

I have often said that I am a dealmaker, not a deal-breaker. If I don't get the deal done, not only does my client lose but so do I. But if the deal is not right, I always have to be prepared to walk away.

This is the single most difficult aspect of dealmaking: As badly as you may want the deal to happen, you have to hold back part of yourself in the event that the gap between you and the other party is too great to ever be closed.

Why? Because of the following paradox: The other side needs to believe you are prepared to walk away so that you don't have to. And the only way you can be completely convincing is to *really* be prepared to walk away if the situation calls for it. This is the best mind-set you can bring with you to the table.

In addition to allowing you to walk away if necessary, it also brings a sense of clarity about the deal itself. And while the vast majority of deals I attempt do get done, there are those rare occasions where I've had to pick up my cards and go home.

When we were looking for a clothing deal for Andy Roddick shortly after he had won the U.S. Open, both Andy and I assumed it was going to be with Nike, because Nike almost always grabbed up the high-profile athletes. Nike is the most ubiquitous brand in sports. Among their endorsees are LeBron James, Tiger Woods, and Roger Federer, who, at the time I was talking to them about Andy, was ranked number one in the world and may very well be one of the best players to ever pick up a tennis racket.

I flew to London to meet with Ian Todd, the chief marketing officer of Nike, who had flown in from France. I didn't think I would get it, but I was prepared to ask for $5 million a year for five years for Andy.

Ian and I met at the Carlton Tower Hotel. After exchanging some pleasantries, Ian reached into his briefcase, pulled out a sheaf of papers that were clipped together, and placed them in front of him. He then rather theatrically pushed these papers across the table and said, "Here's our contract with Roger Federer."

The implication was clear: Since this was the number one player in the world, Andy should expect to get no more than Roger, even though he was an American. But I happened to know what Roger's deal was with Nike, and it was terrible—around $1 million a year for five years with performance bonuses.

If Nike was going to insist on using the Federer contract as the benchmark, then we were in trouble. Under the circumstances, I did the only thing I could do: I pushed Roger's contract back over to Ian without even looking at it and said, "I'm not interested in Roger's deal. I'm interested in the deal for the number one American player. We are thinking five years at $5 million a year."

I knew as soon as I said it that the negotiations were probably over, but I really did feel that the shoe and apparel deal was worth $5 million—although my assumption had also been that our best chance of getting that was going to be from Nike.

We continued to negotiate for about another hour, but it became fairly apparent to both Ian and me that the distance between us was too great to ever close.

So I had to walk away. I had to take all my marbles—or, more accurately, leave all of Nike's marbles on the table—and go home. Andy was the hottest commodity in tennis at that time, and I had already assured him and his parents that we would work out something with Nike. Now I was empty-handed.

I immediately started working the phones, but the tennis merchandising universe is a very small one, and the two remaining major players, Adidas and Reebok, while interested, were not even in the same ballpark as Nike. Now I was left with only the smaller European brands with little American presence such as K-Swiss, Ellesse, and Le Coq Sportif.

That's when I got the idea to call my friends Jean-Claude Fauvet and Bernard Lacoste. Lacoste had had no American presence in tennis for quite some time, but as I've already related in an earlier story, the timing was perfect. They were looking to get back into the American tennis market, and Andy's name had already come up. After a considerable amount of back-and-forth over the next couple of weeks, we were able to get close to the deal we had hoped for.

With Nike not only did I have to be prepared to walk away, but I ultimately had to. And while that ended up making my job immensely more difficult and our situation more precarious, I would do the same thing again. That rare occasion when you walk away is what puts teeth into the other ninety-nine times you don't.

Step 9: Shake Hands

It's important to keep in mind that once the deal is done and you and the other party reach agreement, that's when the relationship really begins. No matter how good a deal you think you have done for yourself, don't let them see it. Shake hands and be gracious. In negotiation, just as in life, politeness counts. And you are playing for the future.

When I think of a lack of graciousness actually costing a client money, it is tennis champion Ivan Lendl who immediately comes to mind. Ivan just didn't get it.

I was once in a board meeting when one of my associates received an "urgent" call from Lendl. We all waited for the associate to return, and when he did, about fifteen minutes later, he said, "You're not going to believe this one. Ivan is in the Toronto airport. He said, 'I'm waiting here at the gate, and the gate attendant is refusing to change my ticket to an aisle seat. Here, I'm going to put her on the phone, and I want you to tell her who I am.'"

It was Ivan's inflated ego and lack of manners that ended up costing him deals. I remember when my associates explained to Ivan that his scowling and grimacing on and off the court were hurting his image and, by extension, his endorsement income.

Ray Benton, the president of ProServ, told him, "Ivan, when you come up to the net to shake hands after the match, if you could just smile and tap the other player on the shoulder, I will guarantee you a million more dollars in endorsements."

Ivan thought for a moment. Then he shook his head and said, "Nah, it's not worth it."

Needless to say, even though he was a great player, he was a tough sell. His rude behavior and bad attitude cost him countless amounts of money.

11

STAY BALANCED

I find it interesting that in the two major individual sports, golf and tennis, the instructions for how to grip the club or the racket are exactly the same: Grip it as though you were holding a bird, not so tight as to choke it but firm enough that it won't fly away. It's a matter of balance—between being too firm and overcompensating by not being firm enough. When our client Andy Roddick went out in one of the early rounds of the 2008 Wimbledon, he gave a quote to the media that was right on the mark. "I wanted to win so badly," he said, "I guess I gripped the racket too tight."

I intentionally made this the last chapter of the book because I wanted to end with the importance of balance. I think the same balance that Andy was looking for applies to dealmaking as well. Don't get too high and don't get too low. Don't be afraid to show your enthusiasm or your desire to make the deal, but don't let your emotions get the best of you and end up saying something you might regret. You can choke a deal just as you can choke a tennis match.

Step Back and Slow Down

Losing your temper or your self-control or putting the other party on the defensive almost never works to your advantage. This is something that invariably occurs in the heat of the moment, of course, and the problem with the heat of the moment is just that, and you'll probably regret emotional actions later.

What you can do, however, is step back from the situation and then slow down in order to put some time and distance between yourself and whatever might be causing the tension. This is a totally unnatural response for some people, so it takes a lot of conscious effort, practice, and discipline. But over time it can be learned.

The most visual depictions of this restraint take place in the world of sports. In tennis, for instance, it's often a matter of stepping back from the service line and taking the fully allotted twenty-five seconds between serves in order to calm your nerves and regain your composure. The best illustration of this is almost certainly Tiger Woods, who has an uncanny ability to step back and slow everything down when the overwhelming temptation is to speed everything up. The greater the pressure, the more deliberate he becomes, repeatedly stepping away from the ball until he has an exact visualization of what he wants to do.

The goal is not to be completely at the mercy of the moment but to achieve some sort of inner calm while simultaneously being at your competitive best. With the greatest athletes the two seem to go hand in hand. Take Tiger Woods again or Michael Jordan or Joe Montana. They have all displayed some kind of inner peace in those moments when the competitive fires were burning at their brightest. The focus they have and the calm they display have the effect of making people trust and admire them.

The most outwardly serene and inwardly competitive person I have ever known—even more so than Michael Jordan—was not even a professional athlete. It was Senator Robert F. Kennedy.

I got to know Bobby, Ethel, and their kids through their love of tennis. They had a court in their backyard, and I was a frequent guest and doubles partner. They were such extraordinary people—so upbeat and positive and joyful—that every time I went there, it felt as if we were celebrating something.

Other than the week when I married Carole and later when my twin daughters, Alexandra and Kristina, were born, the greatest week of my life occurred in March 1968. That same week I was named captain of the U.S. Davis Cup team and then a few days later I was appointed Bobby's lead advance man for five of the western states.

I remember this one incident as if it were yesterday. On March 31, 1968, we had just flown back from a very successful campaign swing through Arizona and had landed on the tarmac at New York's La Guardia Airport. At that time the race was neck and neck between Bobby's legacy and charisma and Lyndon Johnson's incumbency. Once we had pulled into the gate, Bobby asked me to stand in the aisle and block anyone from getting by until Ethel had a chance to go into the bathroom and compose herself. There was tragedy on both sides of the family; Ethel had lost three relatives in plane crashes, so she was terrified of flying and sometimes a nervous wreck by the time we landed.

As I was standing there, this very big person burst through the airplane door and said, "I've got to talk to Senator Kennedy right away." Bobby was sitting just behind me and didn't look up from the paper he was reading, so I said, "I'm sorry. Senator Kennedy is waiting for his wife and can't see anyone right now." Now this guy's eyes were starting to bulge. "Goddamnit!" he said. "Do you know who I am? I am the New York Democratic Party's state chairman. Lyndon Johnson has just withdrawn from the race two hours ago, and I've got twenty thousand people out there waiting to see Senator Kennedy. Do you understand that?"

That was the moment that virtually assured Bobby the Democratic nomination. I knew Bobby had heard him because he was sitting right behind me, and I also knew that *he* knew what this meant. I turned around, and Bobby looked up from the paper he was reading, stared straight at me with those steely blue eyes, nodded, and smiled. Then he went back to reading the paper. That was it. It never came up again. But, at that moment, I believed that Bobby clearly thought he would be president of the United States.

Eventually Ethel and I sneaked out the back of the plane, and as we were walking on the tarmac, heads covered, she said to me,

"Donald, tomorrow all of Jack's people, like Kenneth O'Donnell, Larry O'Brien—they'll all be back to help Bobby, but we'll always remember those people who were with us the first two weeks of the campaign." Of course, neither of us could have foreseen the horrible tragedy that would occur just two months later. I am convinced that if Bobby Kennedy had not met his tragic fate, he would have been the next president and would have changed the course of American history.

Trust Your Instincts

Too many times in the business world, people are so anxious to see the deal happen they will misread or completely ignore their feelings. While it is important to be logical and restrained, you can't ignore your instincts. It is one of the most powerful negotiating tools you have.

I mentioned earlier that I got to know Dean Smith, the coach of UNC's basketball team, by promising not to bother his players in return for face time at the end of the season. In our first visit to the campus, however, Coach Smith had arranged for us to meet with his best senior, Bob McAdoo (who was coming out that year and went on to have a fifteen-year NBA career), because it was already pretty late in the game in terms of that year's draft.

That night I called Coach Smith at home and said, "Bob McAdoo has already signed with someone."

DON'T GET EMOTIONAL

Jonathan Blue

Blue is chairman and managing director of the private equity firm Blue Equity, LLC.

The most important aspect of making a deal is to leave emotion at the door. Emotion can easily overrule logic during negotiations.

The most difficult deal (and the best deal) I've made was the one that taught me the importance of overcoming emotions. I had the opportunity to sell the family business, which was started in 1913, after four generations of success. Having grown up in a household where the family business was discussed at the dinner table made the decision to sell bittersweet.

On paper the deal was great for our family, and accepting the offer would have been an easy decision under any other circumstances. But we all feared the unknown—what we'd do with ourselves without the family business. This led to some resistance on our part. Looking back, I realize that if we hadn't had such a patient and willing buyer, the finalization of the deal may have been jeopardized.

The deal turned out to be one of the best of my career because I was able to build a private investment firm from the revenue. I have been able to repeat the process of building enterprises, selling them, and creating value for partners and team members along the way. ∎

"That's impossible," Coach Smith said. "That's against every rule in my book. Why would you say something like that?"

I answered, "During our whole presentation he kept looking at the ceiling and fidgeting in his seat. He could not have been less interested, and he couldn't wait to get out of there."

As it turned out, McAdoo *had* signed with someone else, and Coach Smith got to the pro team's owner and had him tear up the agreement. But that night I think I began to earn Coach Smith's trust in my judgment. I had not let the prospect of representing McAdoo cloud my instincts. That alerted Coach Smith, which resulted in his getting information about one of his players that he had not known!

It's Your Job to Make It Work

When you're a negotiator, it's up to you to come up with new ways to make things work. You can't always wait around for an advertising guru, a higher-up, or the other side to hand you the solution. When you start thinking creatively but practically, many new doors will open for you.

From the time you begin a deal until the time the deal is done, many circumstances will probably change—sometimes to your advantage, other times maybe not; sometimes because of something you can control, and often because of something over which you have no control. No matter what the circumstances are, it's your job to make the deal work for you. You can't waste your time thinking about what you "normally do." You can definitely get stuck in a rut if you don't get creative. When I finally decided to get creative, I ended up selling my company . . . twice!

The first time was in 1998 when a company called SFX, which owned or controlled all the rock-and-roll tours and music venues in America, made me the proverbial offer I couldn't refuse. ProServ was the first of the fourteen sports management firms that SFX bought, and I agreed to stay on as the senior vice president of the new group, although it was a hollow title because what they really wanted was my Rolodex.

Unbeknownst to anyone, the chief executive and principal shareholder of SFX, Robert Sillerman, was about to sell the company and figured bringing in a few names like Michael Jordan, Jimmy Connors, Boomer Esiason, and Patrick Ewing certainly wasn't going to hurt the sales price.

As Sillerman almost always is, he ended up being right. SFX was sold at a premium to the radio giant Clear Channel, which in turn spun off the concert tours and the sports group as a separate public company, Live Nation.

Otherwise the SFX sports division was something of a disaster. Sports management is highly entrepreneurial. Put a bunch of entrepreneurs together under one umbrella, and what you are going to get is a bunch of entrepreneurs, each going off in his own direction with little regard for the company as a whole.

As it turned out, the new owners agreed with me. This sports division made no sense. I got a call from the CEO of Live Nation, Michael Rapino, who told me the plan was to spin off SFX

Sports as its own entity and to raise money through a private sale. When he told me the kind of money he was looking for, I immediately knew it wasn't going to work. What I didn't know was how that was going to affect me.

In the meantime I had received a call from a young man from Louisville, Kentucky, Jonathan Blue, who had started a very successful private investment company, Blue Equity, and was now looking to get into the sports business as an owner himself. I told him that at the time my hands were tied but things could change and I would stay in touch.

Several months went by before Live Nation got back to me with a status report. As I had anticipated, the private sale had been unsuccessful, and they were now giving me the opportunity to buy back most of my company, ProServ, for a fraction of what I had originally received for it.

That changed everything. One day we were part of their bigger entertainment plans; the next day they didn't want to own us. I knew I had unbelievable leverage because this was, in fact, their Plan B, and there wasn't any Plan C.

I had always imagined that I would continue to head my own company, and this is what I intended to do until I started thinking creatively. As much as I loved being the sole owner, the prospect of being completely responsible for multimillion-dollar overhead again was not appealing. I had never had a partner, but perhaps now was the right time to change that. With that in mind I decided to enter into a partnership with Jonathan Blue. I was even willing to be the minority partner. This new company, now called Blue Entertainment Sports Television (BEST), was

INVEST IN INNOVATION

Philip Geier

Geier was the chairman and chief executive officer of Interpublic for twenty-five years. He currently runs a consulting firm, the Geier Group.

What I find is that the most important aspects of dealmaking fall under the general category of due diligence. This includes the following:

- Knowing the strategic rationale for the acquisition
- Analyzing the acquired company's position in the market relevant to its competitors
- Researching the career histories of the company's management (especially important in cases where start-up ad agencies are being acquired)
- Reviewing financial data, including revenue, profits for the past five years, forward projections, and the full balance sheet for the prior year
- Developing trust

Diligence has got to go deep down and be thorough. For a company to be acquired, its management must be measured by its ability to be trusted and to live up to its commitments. Follow through on the agreement but also establish how the company will help build the business once the deal is done.

In my favorite series of deals, my company, Interpublic, chose to invest in innovation. By the late 1980s, Interpublic realized the growing importance of international TV programming to our clients' global communications strategies. Calculated product placement—placing a product within an appropriate show—was also becoming extremely important. Product placement must not only reinforce a brand's connection with its target audience but also give the client a comfort level with the quality and suitability of the programming that surrounds the brand.

Interpublic saw these trends early. We negotiated the international rights to *Wheel of Fortune* and *Jeopardy!*. From there our Initiative Media subsidiary worked with Lintas Worldwide to package the shows on behalf of our client, Unilever. Unilever's agreement gave it "ownership" in terms of product placement and advertising (with a portion of its advertising sold to local, noncompetitive clients). The shows were wildly popular, becoming nighttime ratings leaders in many markets. Unilever was delighted. It was enjoying tremendous exposure and advertising efficiencies for virtually no risk. Interpublic's first foray into TV programming was an immediate success.

We had been on the leading edge of this new phase of programming innovation, and we used the proceeds to continue investing in new areas. Investing in innovation doesn't always guarantee success. But when it works, you can really strike it rich. ■

not only able to buy back most of ProServ at twenty cents on the dollar but also get back about fifty of our top properties, including forty players' contracts and ten major television properties that included the French Open and the U.S. Open!

This turned out to be the perfect solution for me. I have found Jonathan Blue to be smart, extremely hardworking, and fair-minded. I couldn't ask for more in a partner, and so far my work at BEST has been a very enjoyable experience. Additionally, not only am I free to do deals, I no longer have to look over my shoulder for fear of being second-guessed. Most important, because I did something unusual by taking on a partner, I do not have that big overhead expense to contend with anymore.

Be Fair

I believe in that old adage "If it's too good to be true, then it probably is."

A major part of being balanced is being fair. You don't want to tip the scales too far on one side or the other (including your side), because even if you come out with more than you deserve on one deal, it's likely that others will find out and you'll get a reputation as an unfair person who shouldn't be dealt with. If you persuade someone to make a deal that is very one-sided, there is a good chance the other side won't be able to afford what they agreed to and will simply break the agreement. The other possibility is that the ill will builds up and eventually undermines the deal no matter how many pieces of paper have been signed.

Several years ago, in an effort to boost attendance and income, the ATP established a circuit of ten high-level, big-prize-money tennis tournaments, which they called the Masters series. The ATP had gone to ten major existing tournaments and asked them to get rid of all their television and marketing deals in return for joining the Masters Tour, which guaranteed them all the top-ranking players. In other words, they would have to deliver their courts "clean"—free of any court signage or other promotional references. In return, each tournament would get one-tenth of the income from the TV and marketing rights for these events.

At Wimbledon that year the ATP came to me and asked if I was interested in bidding for the marketing and TV rights. I said, "Of course." Then I heard what they were looking for—$68 million. Since I represented the international TV rights to the French Open and the U.S. Open, I knew what the deal was worth—about two-thirds of the ATP's asking amount. "No, thanks," I said. "I think that price is way over what these rights are worth."

I saw the ATP officials—Larry Scott and Mark Miles—about four months later, and they said, "Everyone except you is bidding—SFX, IMG, Octagon, and a European company, ISL—and we're up to $110 million."

I said, "Please don't accept that deal. That price is so over-inflated, they will never make their money back. It could cause whoever pays that to go under, and then everybody loses. That's not beating someone in an evenly matched game. That's like not having the guy win a single point."

Six months later I heard they had finalized a deal with the European company ISL Worldwide—for one billion dollars over a ten-year period!

Shortly thereafter I received a call from the chairman of ISL, who asked me to have breakfast with him. When we met, he said,

"Donald, I'm very unhappy with you. I hear you have been bad-mouthing the TV deal to everyone."

"That's because I think you've lost your mind," I said. "This deal is going to fail, and it's going to be terrible for professional tennis."

And that's exactly what happened. ISL couldn't sell enough TV rights or get sponsors to pay big enough dollars to cover even a fraction of their costs. They went bankrupt almost immediately and didn't pay the ATP anything other than the $50 million they had already put in escrow.

Now the ten tournaments were reduced to accepting $5 million each—a pittance compared to what it had cost them to give up all their TV and marketing rights.

The ATP had made such a "great" deal for itself that it almost ruined tennis, and it took the sport several years to recover.

Simply put, both you and your opponent need to get something out of the deal you're about to make, and contrary to logic—perhaps a greedy kind of logic—in my experience deals that are equal hold up the best. Equal partnerships, where both sides' voices are heard, work so much better than 49/51, where one person is in a minority. Even when you're not forging partnerships, remember this rule. It will keep you fair and will keep other dealmakers coming back for more mutually and equally beneficial deals.

One of my daughters, Kristina, recently interviewed Bradbury Anderson, the CEO of Best Buy, for an article for *Time* magazine. As you can imagine, Best Buy makes thousands of deals each year, usually involving buying large quantities of electronics. Anderson told Kristina that the only deal he will accept is one that's 50/50 even if the proposed deal was lopsided, to give him *more* than the electronic vendor.

He realizes that he'll have to work with all his vendors countless times in the future, and if the deal doesn't work out well for both parties, that hurts him the next time he has to negotiate with that person on something else. Plus, he said, the people work hardest for everyone involved when they think they've gotten a fair deal. Of course, Best Buy does not accept anything *less* than a 50/50 deal either. You've got to have the confidence to get your fair share, too.

You Can't Please Everybody

Honestly, if everybody you meet adores you, you're doing something wrong. I'm not advocating that you go and make enemies, but it's impossible to please everybody and always look out for your best interest at the same time. This doesn't mean you should constantly be suspicious of people's motives—that would be silly and counterproductive. The important thing, though, is not to be swayed by everything anyone tells you. Keep your value system intact so that you'll always have a home base to work from, and you won't get sucked into anyone else's agenda. When you base your self-worth on others' opinions and needs, you end up at the mercy of their whims.

A while back, a high school teacher from Arizona by the

EVERYBODY WINS

Tom James

James is chairman and chief executive officer of Raymond James Financial, Inc., and chairman of its subsidiary, Raymond James & Associates, Inc.

The most important aspect of a deal is that it needs to be satisfactory to both parties, which implies that each party understands the needs and considerations of the other. As a general rule, most deals that fail do so because the organizational cultures or people didn't mesh. The pre-deal analysis often doesn't contemplate all the details that need to be considered, and buyers often become caught up in the tendency to close in spite of somewhat obvious problems.

The best deal I ever made was to acquire the Financial Services Corporation of America at the end of the financial crisis of the early 1970s. The deal gave us about one hundred top financial planners all over the Southeast during a time when it would have been very expensive to grow our firm with traditional employee offices. What FSC got out of it was to find a home for its brokers while extracting itself from a business it didn't want to be in. That acquisition gave us the financial planners we needed and proved that the independent contractor model could work for us on a larger scale. As a result, we began to recruit nationwide, and RJF grew to become a national firm in a relatively short period of time. ■

name of Les Snyder was about to become the new president (an unpaid position) of the United States Tennis Association (USTA). At the time we represented both foreign and domestic TV rights to the U.S. Open, which provided about 90 percent of the USTA's income and was obviously a huge property for us as well.

On several occasions I tried to make friends with Les, but I found him to be a really cold fish and a know-it-all, not someone I would want to hang out with or even get to know better. Then some of my friends on the USTA board told me Snyder was planning to terminate our domestic television rights. We had done a great job for the USTA, so I didn't believe them. But sure enough, once Snyder had the presidential power, one of his first acts was to give the domestic rights to our chief competitor, IMG.

I was convinced I could get these rights back, but one of my friends on the board told me to forget it. When I asked why, he said, "Because Snyder just doesn't like you."

Sometimes these things happen, and when they do, just shrug them off. You can't please everybody.

Don't Make People Feel Bad

You never know who that intern may be connected to or what he or she will become in the future. For this reason it's best not to abuse your power and make anyone feel bad. But beyond that, making someone feel bad is just bad business. I know what it feels like to be demeaned, and it's something that stays with you a long time.

One of my first jobs out of law school was working for Sargent Shriver, who became my friend and a mentor when he was head of the Office of Economic Opportunity. One day Sarge sent me over to meet with Donald Rumsfeld, who at the time was a very influential Republican congressman, about increasing the funding for the OEO. We knew if we could win over Rumsfeld, another twenty votes would follow him.

Rumsfeld had been an all-American wrestler at Princeton, and I was very good friends with his college roommate, Pablo Eisenberg, so I figured we'd have a lot in common.

But I wasn't in his office three minutes when he said to me, "You're wasting your time. I'm not voting for any more OEO funding." He then did the strangest thing: He jumped up, came around his desk, got right in my face, and said, "Now get the hell out of my office." He's short and powerful, and for a moment I thought he was going to physically throw me out, but then I realized he was just reaching around me to open the door. As I exited the office, he added, "And tell Shriver not to send any more of his PR jocks down here."

Outside his office I turned beet red, but it was a good lesson. I now knew what it felt like to be totally humiliated. Of course, I'm not perfect, and every once in a while I need a sharp reminder, which is what I recently got from someone on the other side of the negotiating table.

I was involved in a major licensing negotiation when a serious misunderstanding came up about the options clause. We had the option to terminate after three years, but they were insisting it was a mutual option—that they had the option to terminate after three years as well.

I had been talking to the other party on the phone for half an hour, and I was becoming increasingly impatient. I thought we had a deal, and now we were getting nowhere. I remember it was a Sunday morning because everything else was so quiet, when suddenly I just exploded: "Goddamnit, I'm not going to turn down every other company to give you this opportunity and then allow you to walk away in three years. It's not going to happen!"

There was absolute silence on the other end of the phone for what seemed like several minutes but was probably around ten seconds. Then, in a very calm voice, the other party said, "Donald, we've had five meetings now, which have all been polite and cordial, and we've always gotten along. But now you're getting nasty. I would really appreciate it if we could just go back to being nice to each other."

I immediately felt embarrassed for the way I had behaved. He was absolutely right, and he had shamed me into realizing it. I apologized and then tried to state my concerns in a different way—and with a different tone of voice.

Eventually we compromised, and we've remained on very cordial terms ever since. We did concede to give them their option but only after five years rather than three. There were also a number of penalties and bonus provisions we obtained if they chose to opt out.

Don't Make People Look Bad

A corollary to not making people feel bad is not making them look stupid either, or, more to the point, *feel* stupid. You would think this would be pretty obvious, but I've seen it happen—and blow deals—more times than I care to remember: Someone starts talking. Then he picks up steam and becomes oblivious to everyone else in the room or to the fact that the more he talks, the more embarrassing or insulting it is to someone else.

I was once in a meeting with the owner and the new general manager of one of the teams in the NBA. I had brought along a younger colleague who was very smart but, as it turned out, not very self-aware. Admittedly, the GM wasn't the sharpest knife in the drawer, but I could see that my colleague, in trying to impress the owner with his knowledge, was starting to make the GM look stupid. The more he talked, the more I could see the GM squirming in his chair and becoming uncomfortable.

After the meeting I said, "Now you have to go back in there and try to get this deal done with the GM. How smart does that make us look?"

When you make someone feel like an idiot, you always run the risk that he's going to feel that way simply because he is dealing with you.

Conclusion

I have a general rule that I apply to books of this sort, which is if I can find five pieces of advice that I can immediately apply to my business, then it has been well worth the price of admission. I hope you have found at least that many negotiating tips on business strategies among these pages that can help you in your own business.

Without a doubt, closing the deal is the "yesss!" moment in business. It is bringing to bear all your knowledge and preparation, all your skills at reading people and reading the situation, to a single focal point. As a former international tennis player, the joy I got from winning a match is no different than the adrenaline rush I get from completing a successful negotiation.

If I could offer one final piece of advice, which is very much in keeping with this chapter, it would be "stay in the moment." Appreciate your surroundings. Stay attuned to the mood in the room. Listen intently, not to what you think someone is about to say, but to what the person is actually saying in real time. That is not only the joy of dealmaking. It is the reward for being successful.

EPILOGUE

EPILOGUE: IT'S ALL ABOUT ATTITUDE

I wrote this book hoping to be informative and helpful to people wanting to learn in business. How to make deals is not really what this book is all about. Dealmaking is actually a study of human nature: observing what drives a person or a company. How do they respond? What do they think?

If dealmaking is the art of negotiating and negotiation is a journey and a process—not a destination or an event—then learning to appreciate your adversaries' sensitivities and viewpoints is critical to a favorable outcome—a successful result in your journey.

But success is an overworked word. It comes in many flavors and often means different things to different people. My favorite definition comes from the poet Bessie A. Stanley: "He has achieved success who has lived well, laughed often, and loved much . . . who has left the world better than he found it, whether by an improved poppy, a perfect poem, or a rescued soul . . . who has always looked for the best in others and given them the best he had."

In my opinion, you never achieve real success unless you *like* what you are doing. That is where your passion and desire come together to produce a meaningful result for your efforts. The joy is in the striving—the seeking of excellence—not in merely winning or losing a deal, but rather in achieving a conclusion that is equally desirable for both sides. This is often hard to achieve but always the best outcome. A "good deal" is one where both parties believe they have achieved at least some of their needs and wishes.

If dealmaking is a study of people and their nature, I have tried in this book to give you suggestions for developing your skills in evaluating those with whom you negotiate. "People skills"—how you approach, learn, understand, and then *react to others*—is the most important aspect of daily living in our busy, complex world. Charles Swindoll says it best, "The longer I live, the more I realize the impact of attitude on life. . . . I am convinced that life is 10% what happens to me, and 90% how I react to it. And so it is with you."

Two of my personal heroes, Sargent Shriver, in service to his country, and Jack Kramer, in service to tennis (the sport I love), both had that rare quality of understanding and empathizing with all types of people naturally, which empowered their strong ability to influence those around them. Both made a *difference* in our society, and so can you. With the right attitude, you can dream it, and, yes, you can do it, because we all are in charge of our attitudes. And so it is with you—start now.

Donald Dell, a graduate of Yale University and the University of Virginia School of Law, is the cofounder of the Association of Tennis Professionals and the founder and CEO of the leading sports agency ProServ. A former player and captain of the U.S. Davis Cup tennis team, Dell was elected to the International Tennis Hall of Fame in 2009. He founded the Washington, D.C., Legg Mason Tennis Classic and has worked as a television tennis commentator on NBC, ESPN, Tennis Channel, and PBS. Early in his career, he worked as a special assistant so Sargent Shriver at the Office of Economic Opportunity (OEO) and then as an advance man in the 1968 presidential campaign of Robert F. Kennedy. Dell currently is the group president of BEST, Inc. (Blue Entertainment Sports Television) and teaches a sports law class at the University of Virginia School of Law. He lives with his wife, Carole, on a farm in Potomac, Maryland.

John Boswell has written or cowritten seventeen books, including the number one *New York Times* bestseller (with Mark McCormack) *What They Don't Teach You at Harvard Business School.* Most recently, he collaborated with David Novak, CEO of Yum! Brands, on *The Education of an Accidental CEO.*

San Diego Public Library
DATE DUE SLIP
****
**

Date due: 10/3/2014,23:59
Title: Sophocles I, Oedipus the
King, Oedipus at Colonus
Call number: 882/SOPHOCLES
Item ID: 31336072084776
Date charged: 8/5/2014,13:44

Total checkouts for session:1
Total checkouts:

<><><><><><><><><><><>
Renew at
www.sandiegolibrary.org
OR Call 619-236-5800 or
858-484-4440 and press 1
then 2 to RENEW. Your
library card is needed to
renew borrowed items.

San Diego Public Library
DATE DUE SLIP
****
**

Date due: 9/19/2014,23:59
Title: Never make the first offer :
(except when you sho
Call number: 658.4052/DELL
Item ID: 31336084855577
Date charged: 8/29/2014,17:22

Date due: 9/19/2014,23:59
Title: Guerrilla negotiating :
unconventional weapons an
Call number: 658.4052/LEVINSON

Item ID: 31336050253351
Date charged: 8/29/2014,17:22

Total checkouts for session:2
Total checkouts:

<><><><><><><><><><><><>
Renew at
www.sandiegolibrary.org
OR Call 619-236-5800 or
858-484-4440 and press 1
then 2 to RENEW. Your
library card is needed to
renew borrowed items.

INDEX

INDEX

INDEX